Science Education in North-Eastern States of India

Science Education in North-Eastern States of India

Ed.

Dr. Nithiya Amirtham S

GYAN

ISBN: 978-81-212-2006-4

Published, 2020

Published by

Gyan Publishing House
5, Ansari Road
Daryaganj, New Delhi-110002
Phone: 011-47034999, 9811692060
www.gyanbooks.com
E-mail: books@gyanbooks.com

Printed at: G. Print Process, Delhi.

Contents

Preface

The idea of publishing a book based on science education in North-Eastern States of India has travelled a long journey. In a related theme, Indian Council of Social Science Research- North Eastern Regional Centre (ICSSR-NERC) sponsored national seminar was organized in November 2018 at Department of Education, Mizoram University, Aizawl, India which paved the path to the emergence of this book. The thought of bringing out a book based on the discussions and empirical researches in science education area in north-eastern states was felt as a necessity to provide insights and to encourage more explorations.

A good number of quality papers have been picked out from the seminar papers in-addition with the papers of researchers who could not participate. The main concern of this book is, to provide varied perspectives towards the prevailing status and issues in science education from school to higher education along with the roles played by various agencies working towards promotion and improvement of science education. Research works conducted in this area requires limelight as it is observed that there is a need for more studies in different angles to provide quality support in improvement of science education in North-Eastern Region of India.

It is expected that this book would furnish the foundations in science education area in North- Eastern States of India with an expectation that it would serve as a beacon to encourage more researches and writings in this area.

Dr. Nithiya Amirtham S

Acknowledgement

The editor expresses gratitude to Prof. R.P.Vadhera, Pro-Vice Chancellor, Mizoram University, Aizawl for sharing his expertise in the area of science education. The editor is thankful to Prof. Poonam Agrawal, Professor and Former Head of Department of Gender Studies, National Council of Educational Research and Training (NCERT), New Delhi for writing the opening chapter. I am grateful to all the chapter contributors from across the North-Eastern States of India for their inputs and their dedications in publishing the book. The editor expresses sincere thanks to Indian Council of Social Science Research-North Eastern Regional Centre (ICSSR-NERC), Shillong and Mizoram University, Aizawl for financial support to organise a national seminar on 'Science Education in North-Eastern States of India: Current Status and Future Directions'. Without the seminar the collection of papers published in this book would not have emerged. My special thanks to the publisher in producing this book. My sincere thanks go to all those who supported me in publishing this book.

Dr. Nithiya Amirtham S

List of Abbreviation

AEQ	:	Academic Emotions Questionnaire
AICTE	:	All India Council for Technical Education
ATS	:	Achievement Test in Science
ESS	:	Emotional Stability Scale
FFM	:	Five Factor Model
GER	:	Gross Enrolment Ratio
GPI	:	Gender Parity Index
ICTs	:	Information and Communication Technologies
IIT	:	Indian Institute of Technology
ISC	:	Indian Science Congress
MBSE	:	Mizoram Board of School Education
MSC	:	Mizoram Science Centre
MSE	:	Mobile Science Exhibition
NCSM	:	National Council of Science Museums
NEI	:	North East India
NPE	:	National Policy on Education
OBCs	:	Other Backward Classes
PCI	:	Pharmacy Council of India
SCs	:	Scheduled Castes
SEL	:	Social and Emotional Learning
STEM	:	Science, Technology, Engineering and Mathematics
STs	:	Scheduled Tribes

List of Tables

List of Figures

Chapter - I

What will Accelerate the Journey? Gender and Science Education with Reference to North-East India

— *Poonam Agrawal*

Introduction

Consensus is emerging among policy makers and economists that at least half of the economic growth in countries is directly attributable to science and technology. Definitely, science education and its appropriate application is a must for a better tomorrow. Besides issues which are obviously directly connected to science e.g. health and wellness, environment, agriculture; there is hardly any social problem on which science cannot make some contribution, be it hunger, poverty, food security, sustainable energy solutions – the spectrum covers all!

For transforming the country as modern India, science was always considered imperative. Science and development were inseparable in the thinking process of our great leaders and thinkers. The Science Policy Resolution, 1958 holds a strong standing as it was the government's stand on promotion of science. The resolution projected science as key to national and individual prosperity when it stated "It is only through the scientific approach and method and the use of scientific knowledge that reasonable material and cultural amenities and services can be provided for every member of the community". The resolution further envisioned that education in science and its application (technology) will give a new dynamism to civilisation by widening the horizons of thinking.

Today India has earned high global respect in science. India is one of the top-ranking countries in the field of basic research. A Nature Index Analysis, 2019, reveals India's high quality research output in global context. Particularly, India's achievements are commendable in chemistry and physical sciences. In chemistry, our country's top institutions are comparable to not only those in Asia but also with those in Europe and USA and are among the top ranking institutions in the world. In space research, India's laurels are incomparable (Kogleck et al., 2015).

From the launch of her first satellite in 1975 to the Mar's mission (*Mangalyaan* and Mission moon (*Chandrayaan*) the journey has been spectacular. India was recognised by NASA as the first to evidence presence of water on moon. The success of Mangalyaan, the cheapest mission of its kind is globally acclaimed. Indian scientists are leading a global project on the Human Proteome Map, the protein equivalent of human genome project.

These are only few of the many examples that have earned India her niche in the global space of science research. But this has not happened overnight. Policy support, inter alia, both for science education and gender equality, has been a crucial driving force in achieving the status that we have today.

Policy Support for Science Education and Gender Equality in Science

The vision of the resolution on promotion of science was reflected in our national policies of education. Consequently, the very first National Policy on Education (NPE, 1968) placed a clear-cut emphasis on science. The Government resolved to promote education in accordance with 17 principles, science education and research was one of them. This was also a reason for giving English learning a place of importance in the curriculum as the policy makers were of the view "study of English should be specially strengthened so as to keep abreast of world knowledge and excel in field of science and technology". While recognising role of science education and research in catalysing the national growth and boosting economy, a very important recommendation was made. This was recommendation of a common curriculum i.e. every child, both boys and girls should study Science and mathematics till the end of the school stage. This paved way for non-discrimination in the education of boys and girls and gave girls an opportunity to be scientists, technocrats and innovators.

In the subsequent National Policy on Education (NPE, 1986) many of the recommendations of the 1968 policy were endorsed, the most important being the continuance of common core curriculum for 10 years of school education, i.e. science remained a compulsory subject for all students till class tenth. The vision was to give sufficient exposure and orientation to all youngsters in every area of knowledge, creativity and exploration, so that they can make informed choice when deciding their education verticals and career choices. The government aimed at promoting science not for just a few with special intellect but as an exciting subject for all.

Women's Legacy in Education in Modern India

Education was viewed as a major instrument of social change and transformation. Modern education for women in India began in the early years of the nineteenth century and by the 1880s universities started admitting them. India has a rich legacy of eminent women in different fields. Savitribai Phule was among the pioneers of women's education in India. Vijaya Lakshmi Pandit was the first Indian woman to hold a cabinet post. She was also India's ambassador to Russia during the late forties. Hansaben Mehta, as early as in 1946, not only became a Vice Chancellor, but could make outstanding contributions to the development of education in India.

Women in Science

In ancient India, Leelavati, the daughter of great Mathematician Bhaskaracharya was herself said to be an accomplished mathematician and astrologer. In pre independent India, Kadambini Ganguly graduated in medicine in 1886 from the Calcutta Medical College and holds the distinction of being the first female graduate and physician of South Asia to be trained in western medicine. Anandibai Joshi is another female physician of Indian origin but she studied and graduated with a degree in medicine in the United States, thus is regarded as the first South Asian female physician to be trained in the tradition of Western medicine abroad. Janaki Ammal obtained a degree in botany in early 1920s when botany was not considered a suitable subject for women. She not only pursued her career in botany but is well known for her research work in cytogenetics. She became the Director-General of the Botanical Survey of India and was awarded Padma Shri in 1977. Relatively more recently Anna Mani earned her laurels as an Indian physicist and meteorologist and made significant contributions in the field of meteorological instrumentation. She is known for her work on solar radiation and retired as Deputy Director General of the Indian Meteorological Department. She was awarded the K.R. Ramanathan Medal in 1987. Kamala Sohonie, the first female student of Prof. CV Raman, also has the distinction of being the first Indian woman to earn a Ph.D. degree in science. Asima Chatterjee is an Indian chemist, highly reputed for her research in the fields of organic chemistry and phytochemistry, anti-cancer alkaloids and for the development of anti-epileptic and anti-malarial drugs. Rajeshwari Chatterjee is regarded as the first woman engineer. Having obtained her degree in Electrical Engineering abroad, she worked in one of the most celebrated science institutes in India, the Indian Institute of Science, Bangalore, when she was the only woman faculty in the institute.

She has to her credit pioneering work on microwave engineering and Antennae Engineering in India and chairperson of the Department of Electro-Communication Engineering, Indian Institute of Science, Bangalore (now Bengaluru).

In modern India, many more women in science have earned top places and high respect not only nationally but globally. Who can forget Kalpana Chawla, the first astronaut of Indian origin to be chosen for NASA's space mission 'Columbia' and later her successor Sunita Williams nee Pandya, who set the record of the longest cumulative spacewalk time by a female astronaut. Other women scientists contributing significantly in NASA projects include Dr. Anita Sengupta, Project Manager at Jet Propulsion Laboratory who designed the 70 foot parachute that slowed the descent of the Curiosity Rover into Mars in 2012 and then got a breakthrough in creating a state of matter called the Bose-Einstein Condensate for NASA's Cold Atom Laboratory. One cannot miss Dr. Madhulika Guhathakurta, who is a product of University of Delhi having earned her Master's degree in Astrophysics. She has directed many science programs but the most celebrated laurel is as *Lead Program Scientist for* The World's First Mission To The Sun - NASA's study of the Sun and its effect on the Solar System (Homegrown, 2017). Dr. Sunetra Gupta, an expert in Theoretical Epidemiology studies infectious diseases using mathematical models. Her contributions have been recognised widely, she is recipient of the scientific medal awarded by the zoological society of London and the Royal Society Rosalind Franklin award (Jadeja, 2015).

In India, women have earned several laurels in space research. The most recent Chandrayaan 2 project was headed by two women scientists.

In other fields, Dr. Indira Hinduja is known for her achievements on in Vitro Fertilisation and Embryo Transfer. Kiran Mazumdar Shaw, the Chairman & Managing Director of a Bangalore based bio-technology company 'Biocon Limited' is a role model for many budding entrepreneurs. Having started her company in the garage of her rented house with a seed capital of Rs. 10,000 has now led this company to a net worth of more than $ 900 million. The Biocon limited produces drugs for cancer, diabetes and auto-immune diseases. She is on the Forbes list of the world's 100 most powerful women and in business list on top 50 women released by the *Financial Times*'.

Dr. Aditi Pant, an oceanographer, after taking her Bachelor's degree from Pune went abroad for further studies. She holds the distinction of being the first Indian woman to visit Antarctica to study Geology and Oceanography (Education World, n.d.). Eight women scientists of India who made history and Satyajit N. Singh is Public Relation Officer at National Council of Science Museums (NCSM) Blog Indian Women in Science & Technology (Singh, 2015). Today the list is quite long of women scientists, technocrats and entrepreneurs in India who are immensely contributing to the advancement of these domains as well to the economy of the nation.

For anyone to be successful in any career and create a niche for oneself, a sound educational foundation is crucial, in which the education in early years of life (in organised structure, referred to as the school education) lays the basis and is expected to create conceptual understanding on which lay the future creativity, explorations and innovations guided by the higher level learning (higher education). Thus, quality education for all, irrespective of any discrimination be it gender or others, is the aim in most countries including India.

Gender Equality in School Education

Continued support to girls' education and empowerment through constitution, policies, plans, programs and incentives has bridged the gender gap over the past decade. As can be seen from the tables below the gender gap in enrolment at school level and retention has been bridged (Table 1.1, 1.2). There is a little gap when it comes to higher education.

Table 1.1: Gender Parity Index (GPI) in India for All Categories of Students for Elementary Level

Year	*Primary (I-V)*	*Upper Primary (VI-VIII)*	*Elementary (I-VIII)*
2010-11	1.01	0.95	0.99
2011-12	1.01	0.99	1.00
2012-13*	1.02	1.05	1.03
2013-14*	1.03	1.08	1.04
2014-15*	1.03	1.09	1.05

*Figures are provisional;

Source: Educational Statistics at a Glance of MHRD, 2016.

Table 1.2: Gender Parity Index (GPI) in India for All Categories of Students for Higher Levels

Level/Year	*Secondary (IX-X)*	*Senior Secondary (XI-XII)*	*(IX-XII)*	*Higher Education*
2010-11	0.88	0.86	0.87	0.86
2011-12	0.93	0.92	0.93	0.88
2012-13*	0.96	0.94	0.99	0.89
2013-14*	1.00	0.98	1.00	0.92
2014-15*	1.01	0.99	1.01	0.92

* Figures are provisional;

Source: Educational Statistics at a Glance of MHRD, 2016.

Higher Education in India- A Glance

According to All India Survey on Higher Education (AISHE), Ministry of Human Resource and Development, Government of India (2018-19), there are a total of 993 Universities (394 Universities are located in rural area), 39931 Colleges (60.53% Colleges are located in Rural Area) and 10725 Stand Alone Institutions listed on the AISHE web portal. In 2017-18, these figures were 903 Universities, 39050 Colleges and 10011 Stand Alone Institutions listed on AISHE web portal, out of these 60.48% colleges were located in rural area.11.04% colleges were exclusively for women. 11.04% Colleges are exclusively for Female. Institutes of high repute are being extended now from tier 1 cities only to other cities. Till 1990s, only 5 Indian Institute of Technologies (IITs) were there in Kharagpur, Bombay, Madras, Kanpur and Delhi but now we have more than 20 IITs, including the ones in Jammu, Ropar, Mandi etc. Thus there are efforts to extend the reach of good quality higher education in rural areas and smaller cities, which will be especially beneficial for women as many a time parents are reluctant to send them to faraway places. However similar attention needs to be paid for institutes of science education and research on the lines and repute of the Indian Institute of Science, Bangalore.

Estimated Gross Enrolment Ratio (GER) in Higher education in India is 26.3%, which is calculated for 18-23 years of age group. Gender Parity Index (GPI) shows that Female participation in Higher Education for All Categories is 100 per 100. GER for male population at all India level is 26.3% whereas for females it is 26.4% (AISHE 2019). Total enrolment in higher education in the last report was estimated to be 36.6 million with 19.2 million boys and 17.4 million girls. Girls constituted 47.6% of the total enrolment.

Gross Enrolment Ratio (GER) in Higher education in India was 25.8%. GER for male population was 26.3% and for females, it was 25.4%. The overall gender parity index in higher education is improving with every year. In 2015-16 it was 0.92, in 2016-17 it was 0.94 and in 2017-18 it reached to be 0.97. And in the latest report, it can be observed that the gender gap exists no more! The gender distribution at different levels of higher education (Fig. 1.1) shows that there are more females than males in certificate courses, post graduation and M.Phil. course; however more males pursue Ph.D. than females.

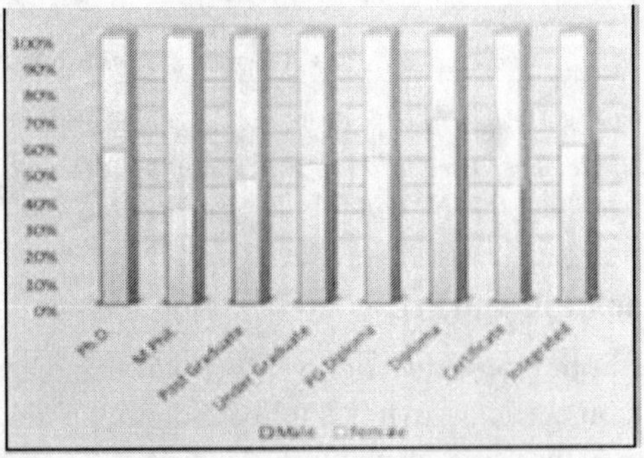

Source: MHRD (2018): AISHE (2017-18) Report.

Fig. 1.1: Gender Distribution at Different Levels of Higher Education in India.

Taking a look at the Male-Female ratio at each level in the latest report (AISHE 2019) reveals the same trend. This may be because of more women are in unorganised sector; therefore certificate courses may be more useful requiring less time duration. Also may be less women pursue Ph.D. after M. Phil. due to time, finance and family constraints. But as Ph.D. is now essential for faculty positions, their participation on these positions would get adversely affected. At all India level the proportion of female faculty (including professors, associate professors and assistant professors) is 40%. The gender distribution in enrolment (Fig. 1.2) in different types of education institutions at undergraduate level shows that with respect to professional courses there is not much difference in the choice of type of institutions between girls and boys as 76.6% of enrolment of girls is either in private or government aided institutions while this figure for boys is 77.4; exhibiting hardly any gender gap.

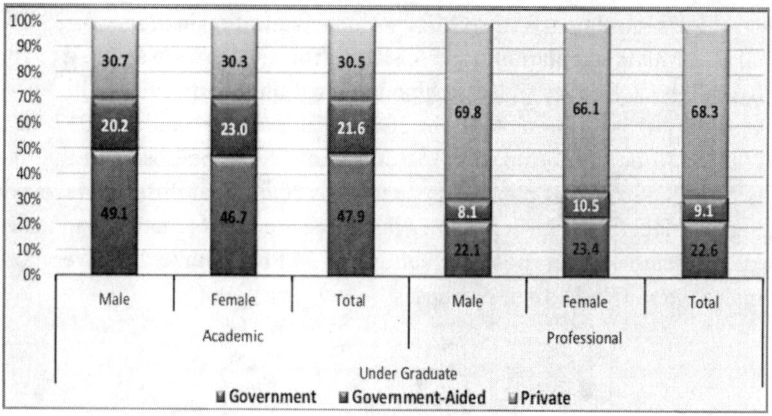

Source: MHRD (2018): AISHE (2017-18) Report.

Fig. 1.2: Gender Distribution in Enrolment in Different Types of Educational Institutions at Undergraduate Level in India

Science Education and Girls

The National Policy on Education (NPE, 1968), India introduced ten years of common curriculum, this implied that each child irrespective of gender will study the same curriculum, also that of Science, mathematics and technology for the ten years of school education. This was further reiterated in the NPE, 1986. This policy has had a long lasting effect in generating women scientists and technocrats as this created interest of girls in these areas gave them an opportunity to prove themselves in these domains and led to generation of awareness and faith among parents and in the society that girls too can excel in these areas. The success of women in these domains has broken many a myths that women's brain is not made for these and that they are suitable for art, language and social sciences only.

At NCERT we are constantly aiming at removing gender bias and bringing equality through our text books and other material in science, mathematics and technology. We also conduct gender auditing of teaching learning material for this purpose. In our training programs also we constantly address this issue. The department has prepared motivational material on women scientists and inventors from the field of science and technology. The KGBV bridge course in science has included brief about women scientists and mathematicians to motivate girls to be scientists and technocrats. The text books of Science addresses gender concerns like who determines the sex of the child, role of women in environment conservation .The training material for teacher educators has a module on gender, science and technology.

The National Focus Group Paper of NCERT on Gender Issues in Education clearly highlights the points to bring gender equality through teaching of Science, Mathematics and technology. The total enrolment at Undergraduate Level in major discipline/subject based on actual response reveals that Science is second major stream with 47.13 lakhs student out of which 49% are male and 51% are female (AISHE 2018-19). Thus the actual data is breaking quite a few myths. One is that students are no more preferring science in view of career opportunities in commerce. But the data proves that after arts, science remains the most preferred domain even for the current generation while the commerce occupies the third preference. Secondly and even more importantly, the general perception is that science is still projected to be a 'man's domain'! But the data evidences that there are more girls in science than boys. This trend was also reported several years back in the AISHE 2011-12 itself. A report of the MHRD (2013) based on AISHE 2011-12 data revealed that girls in Science were more than boys, as the percentage enrolment of boys in Master of Science was 1.71 while that for girls it was 2.46, in engineering for boys it was 0.26 and for girls it was only slightly less i.e. 0.23. As per the latest data, which also confirms the trend of past years, in medical Science stream higher number of female students can be seen, where in out of total 11.96 lakhs students, female students are 7.25 lakhs.

Fig. 1.3 shows Gender wise enrolment at P.G., M.Phil. and Ph.D., level in major disciplines/ subjects. It can be seen that contrary to the general belief there are far more girls than boys in science also at post graduate level. This may be because medical is considered to be a good option for girls; hence those girls who do not get admission in medical continue their higher studies in science.

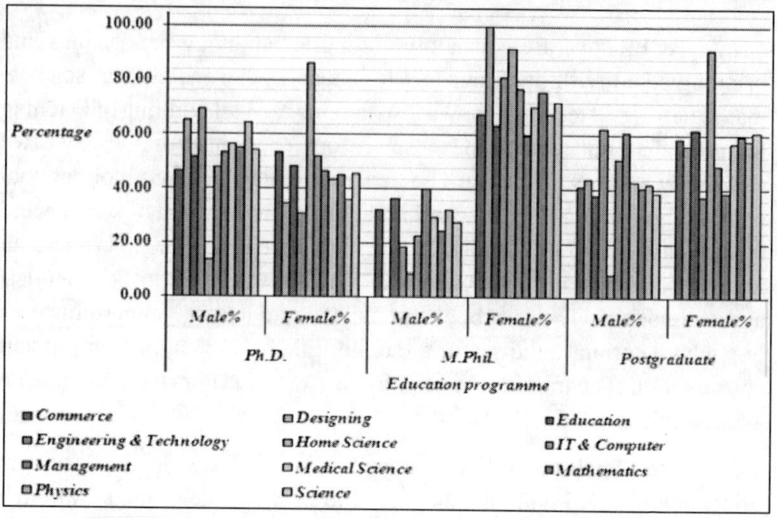

Source: MHRD (2018): AISHE (2017-18) Report.

Fig. 1.3: Gender Wise Enrolment at Ph.D., M.Phil. and P.G Level in Major Disciplines/ Subjects

Further probe reveals that in subjects like mathematics, statistics and physics, which were once considered 'a man's domain' also there are more girls than boys. This could be because currently more girls are aspiring to take professions in engineering and technology, but due to fierce competition they are not getting admission and hence, they pursue mathematics, statistics and physics etc. at P.G. level in universities and colleges where there is less competition. Confirming this view one can see that there are more girls in medical sciences and less in engineering and technology. Share of female students is lowest in Institutions of National Importance e.g. Indian Institutes of Technology (IIT), however recently initiatives have been taken to enhance their participation.

Science Education in North East at School Level

The analysis of data from the National Achievement Survey (NCERT-NAS, 2017) for class X conducted by the NCERT reveals that there is hardly any gap in scores pertaining to science as a subject in the North Eastern states except Tripura where girls have scored marginally less (41) than boys (42). In all other states, Arunachal Pradesh, Assam, Manipur and Mizoram no gender gap is visible as scores are same for girls and boys, i.e. 34, 50, 43 and 33 respectively. In three states, Nagaland, Sikkim and Meghalaya girls have even outperformed boys, the figures for boys and girls being 34 and 35, 37 and 38 and 35 and 36, respectively. At national level also no gender gap has been reported with both boys and girls scoring 44. However, on the whole the performance of North Eastern students is far below than score for the national average (44) with the exception of Assam (50) and Manipur is close (43). Much less is scored by Arunachal Pradesh, Mizoram, Nagaland and Sikkim with the scores being 34, 33, 34.5 and 37.8. On the whole average score of all the North Eastern states together is 38.5 for boys and 38.75 for girls.

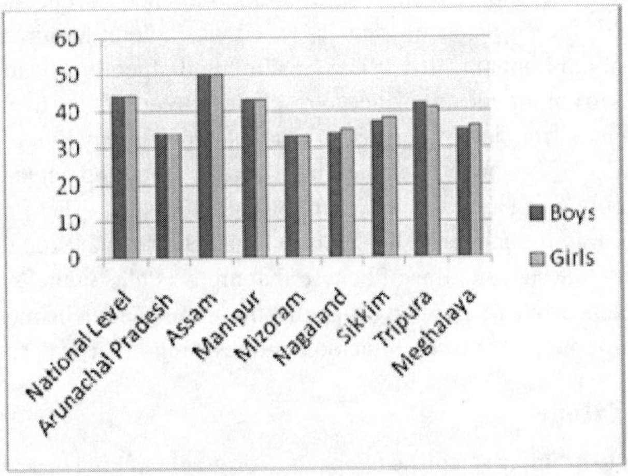

Source: NCERT National Achievement Survey (2017).

Fig. 1.4: State Wise Results of NCERT-National Achievement Survey (2017) in Science for Class X

Thus, the latest data reveals that the North Eastern states need to seriously think to improve the quality and performance of students with respect to science subject. As Assam is performing better than the national average, a detailed study of science education in Assam could probably benefit the other states in the North East, besides taking innovative steps on their own.

Science Education in North East at Tertiary Level

Reports and studies are available which indicate that North Eastern region is not keeping pace with the rest of the nation in Science and Mathematics education (Bala, 2016; Times of India, 2017). The reasons cited are, inter alia, lack of infrastructure. The situation doesn't seem to have changed despite this realization. The AISHE (2018-19) records that there is no specialization university in North East in Science and medical, with the only exception of a medical institute in Assam. Lack of infrastructure and inter-ethnic conflicts compel the youth from the North East to leave their state and migrate.

Among the Science and Technology issues specific to the North Eastern Region, those impressed upon in the Indian Science Congress, 2008 included conservation and protection of biodiversity; establishing models of bio-villages; protection and utilization of indigenous knowledge and organising capacity building programs in science education. 105th Session of Indian Science Congress (ISC) was held at Manipur Central University in Imphal in 2018. The session highlighted to develop simple methods to communicate science to reach the unreached and to encourage use and interpretation of Science principles in day to day living. While it is a matter of honor to host such high level events, the actual benefits accrue only when the resolutions are brought to reality. These definitely pave the way for achieving the goals but the actual steps taken thereafter determine the success. It is of benefit that all the states in the North East have Science and Technology Councils, but these need to be more active on development of science education and research in the states.

Rays of Hope

In order to promote scientific temper and original thinking in school kids, a programme is underway in remote areas of the Northeast. Children are shown a series of short films on a range of subjects, and then a quiz competition is held along with hands-on activities. The initiative called, Sci-Connect, has been undertaken in all the states in the region by Vigyan Prasar (Times of India, 2017). A good success model seems to be available in the northeast itself, as the students' performance in science in Assam has been found to be surpassing the national average (NCERT-NAS, 2017). Sure there would be more initiatives scattered in the whole region which need to be carefully studied, highlighted, disseminated and replicated.

Way Forward

Since the North Eastern region has immense ethnic, socio-cultural and environmental diversity, micro-planning for enhancement of scientific interest, performance and practice could bring better dividends. For education to be attractive and of rich quality; good infrastructure including latest generation laboratories for experimentation, updated faculty and pedagogy facilitating experiential learning are inevitable. Strengthening science education at all levels will be necessary, with specific plans for school and higher level. Synergy with other domains of knowledge and practice is projected as one of the approaches in teaching-learning of science. Networking and Public-Private partnerships, access to national and global resources were never as crucial as in modern days and possible too with the use of technology. North East has unmatched treasure on indigenous knowledge which has to be conserved and tapped to develop sustainable strategies. One has to remember complex is not always successful. Many achievements are results of small and simple steps. The need is to have a whiteboard, sketch problems local to specific regions of the North East and make a roadmap that will accelerate the journey to be leading in science education, exploration and innovations. Failures are to be celebrated to evolve! The key is not to stop, learn, and change the gear and surge ahead.

References

Education World. (n.d.). *Eight women scientists of India who made history*. Retrieved from https://www.educationworld.in/eight-women-scientists-of-india-who-made-history/

Homegrown. (2017, March 13). *Here are 9 Indian NASA scientists you should know*. Retrieved from https://homegrown.co.in/article/800366/here-are-8-indian-nasa-scientists-you-should-know

Jadeja, N. (2015). *7 Incredibly smart Indian women scientists who make us all proud*. Retrieved from https://www.thebetterindia.com/21548/indian-women-scientists-list/

Kogleck et al. (2015). *Indian science ascending: A nature index analysis*. Macmillan Publishers Inc. Sydney: Australia.

MHRD. (2013). *Annual Report (2006-07)*. Department of Higher Education, Ministry of Human Resource Development, Government of India. Retrieved from: https://mhrd.gov.in/sites/upload_files/mhrd/files/document-reports.pdf).

MHRD. (2018). *All India Survey on Higher Education (AISHE) (2017-18)*. Department of Higher Education, Ministry of Human Resource Development, Government of India. Retrived from http://aishe.nic.in/aishe/viewDocument.action;jsessionid=AE01385F5BC2B076606EDA5C5929A0A2?documentId=245).

National Policy on Education (1968). Ministry of Education, GOI. New Delhi.

National Policy on Education (1986). Ministry of Human Resource Development, GOI, New Delhi.

NCERT-NAS (2017). Retrieved from www.ncert.nic.in/programmes/nas/nas.html.

Scientific Policy Resolution. (1958, March 4). No. 131/CF/57, Government of India, New Delhi.

Times of India (2017, October 24). *Northeast states lagging behind in science, mathematics: Report*. Retrieved from https://timesofindia.indiatimes.com/city/itanagar/northeast-states-lagging-behind-in-science-mathematics report/articleshow/61195759.cms? utm_ source=contentofinterest&utm_medium=text&utm_campaign=cppst

Singh, S.N. (2016). Indian women in science & technology [Blog post]. Retrieved from https://ncsm.gov.in/indian-women-in-science-technology/

Chapter - II

Understanding the Status of Science Education at Higher Secondary Level in the North-Eastern States of India: An Analysis from U-DISE Data

—Amardeep Kumar

Introduction

Scientific progress is hallmark of growth and development of any society and country. Scientific temper helps individual and society in fighting against superstitious belief, ignorance, strengthen the spirits of enquiry and experimentation, analytical skills and rational thinking. Science education has been one of the most important study areas of the study in schools itself and continues to be at higher education around the world. Science education helps individual's in problem-solving, critical thinking as lifelong skills. The basic purpose of the science education is to not only promote the scientific and technological development in the overall development of the country and economy but also providing individual's the opportunity to make an informed decision on various issues including scientific and technological issues. Because of its unique strength science has been privileged subjects in the institutions as well as in the society as it is widely persist assumptions that science would improve the standard of life of humans and well-beings.

India is one of the most diversified countries in the worlds in terms of various socio- economic, religious, ethnic and regional grounds. Similarly, educational enrolments are diverse on the above categorisation. In academic discourse, regional aspects are less studied area. North-East states are most diversified region in India on various grounds in general and education particularly. The current chapter discusses the status of science education in the North-East region in India.

Role of Science in Modern World

With rapid industrial growth and development, human beings are increasingly facing the challenges of rapid technological transformations, problems of climate changes, lack of quality education in vast numbers of developing countries, malnutrition among the children at global level, national level and local levels, problems of an ageing population, of environmental degradation. Science plays a vital role in improving the conditions of human lives and well-being.

Incheon Declaration and Framework for Action for the implementation of Sustainable Development Goals 4 on education clearly mentions its commitment to strengthening science, technology and innovation in schoolings and emphasizes that how the use of Information and communication technologies (ICTs) may strengthen education systems, knowledge dissemination, information access, quality and effective learning. Life cannot be imagined without science and technology in the modern world. Scientific enquiry has to be transacted in schooling itself to enhance the interests of the students for innovation in fields of science and technology. The Incheon Declaration on SDG4 mentions that a focus on quality and innovation will require strengthening Science, Technology, Engineering and Mathematics (STEM) at different levels of education. Rapid industrialisation with liberalisation and globalisation has further shown us that without scientific growth and developments a nation cannot sustain for a long in the highly competitive globalised world. Despite the growing importance of science and technology in all facets of human life across the societies, many young people appear to lose their interest for it in schools. This happens not only in developed society but also in developing society like India. It has been observed that this disenchantment with science at schools further led into the higher education.

Diversity and Equity in Science Education: Caste, Class, Gender and Regional Issues

Diversity in science refers to cultivating talent and promoting the full inclusion in access and participation of all the social groups. This includes people from disadvantaged backgrounds those are traditionally underrepresented. Diversity and equity in sciences have been major challenges at global, national and local levels at different levels of education. Diversity is all about the inclusion of people who have been traditionally under-represented in Indian context. It is great challenges for the country like India to aspire for equity and justice in science education. Diversity also influences science teaching, learning and research. It is also accepted by the policy makers that the students from underrepresented communities like Scheduled Castes (SCs), Scheduled Tribes (STs), Other Backward Classes (OBCs) and Minority continuously face challenges not only in access but also in participation at different levels of education in general and at higher secondary level in particularly. It is also a denial of opportunities in participating in sciences education. Equity in science education requires providing equitable access to schooling, science labs, well-trained teachers and motivating and learning environment. However this study is geographically limited to the north-east states of India

North-Eastern States of India- Context

North-Eastern States comprise of eight states; Arunachal Pradesh, Assam, Manipur, Meghalaya, Mizoram, Nagaland, Sikkim and Tripura located in eastern range of the Himalayas. These each state has very distinct cultural and historical uniqueness in terms of languages, ethnicity, communities, cultures, flora and faunas etc. North-East is a multicultural society. As per government report, North-Eastern States total geographical area is 2,62,179 Km^2 which is equal to 8% of the country's total geographical area. The population of these states is 45,587,982 as per 2011 Census which is 3.1% of the country's total population according to the 2011 census. The region has more than 200 tribal groups out 635 tribal groups in the country. These states have special importance for India, not only because of their locations and its diversities but also because of its connectedness to south-east Asian nations. These states work as the passage to south-east Asian countries. These states cover 5000 Km international borders with different neighbouring countries like Myanmar, Bhutan, Bangladesh and China. According to the government of India, Human development Indexes among these states differs and these states are located at different levels. Mizoram, Manipur and Nagaland are on the top of the human development index and other states are at the bottom among these states.

Literacy in North-East States

North-East States have relative fairer literacy rate in terms of comparison with the national literacy rate of 74%. Mizoram has highest literacy rate just after Kerala among the Indian States. However, Tripura having 87.75% of literacy rate which is also much higher than the national average of literacy rate. Sikkim has 82.2%, Nagaland 80.11%, Manipur 79.85%, followed by Meghalaya 75.48%, Assam 73.18% and Arunachal Pradesh 66.95%. It is believed that the spread of Christianity in the North-East region in general and Mizoram, in particular,has made literacy rate better in promoting by promoting school education in the state. Out of the eight states in the region, six states have better literacy rate than the national average. Early awareness of importance for education among the people also equipped to demand better education from the government.

Methodology

The current study uses the Census data 2011 for the general information on literacy rates and U-DISE data has been used for analysing the status of Science education in the North-Eastern States Arunachal Pradesh, Assam, Manipur, Meghalaya, Mizoram, Nagaland, Sikkim and Tripura. With the help of both the data sources, the study tries to understand the nature of participation in science education in the north-east state at higher secondary levels in terms of enrolment in various years. Simple Ranking has been used to rank the states in terms of literacy rates. The passed-out students' data has been taken for only one the year 2017-2018 from U-DISE to understand the pass our percentage at higher secondary levels in North-East States. The purpose of the study is to understand the science education status at the higher secondary levels of schooling with the help of available datasets provided by the U-DISE. Higher secondary level is considered a bridge between the higher education and school education. The subject chosen at this level more or less decides the choice of the subject chosen at higher education. So it is important to understand how exclusion or inclusion takes place before Science education in higher education.

Findings

Table 2.1 shows that literacy rates among the different north-east states of India. Mizoram has highest literacy rates and Assam has the lowest literacy rates among the north east states of India. Assam has even lower than the national average literacy rates.

Table 2.1: Literacy Rate in the North East States (2011)

State	*Literacy Rate (%)*	*Ranks*
Arunachal Pradesh	66.95	8
Assam	73.18	7
Manipur	79.85	5
Meghalaya	75.48	6
Mizoram	91.58	1
Nagaland	80.11	4
Sikkim	82.2	3
Tripura	87.75	2
All India	74.04	

Source: Census, 2011.

This section (Table 2.2) deals with issue of literacy rate based on gender. Gendered Rank is also not very much different among the north-east states in literacy rate as per the census, 2011 expect Meghalaya and Nagaland. Mizoram stands the first rand in literacy rate with both Males and Females literacy rates followed by the Tripura. Sikkim stands the third rank in male literacy however in female literacy Nagaland occupies the third rank. Manipur stand for forth rank in male literacy however Sikkim occupies the fourth rank in female literacy rates. Nagaland stand on the fifth rank in male literacy and in female literacy, it is Meghalaya at fifth rank. Assam stand at sixth ran, Meghalaya at seventh and Arunachal Pradesh occupies the eighth rank in male literacy, however, in female literacy, Manipur stands at sixth, Assam at seventh and Arunachal Pradesh at the eighth.

Table 2.2: Ranking of North-East States Based on Literacy Rate and Gender (2011)

States	*Males*	*Rank*	*Females*	*Rank*
ArunachalPradesh	73.69	8	59.57	8
Assam	78.81	6	67.27	7
Manipur	86.49	4	73.17	6
Meghalaya	77.17	7	73.78	5
Mizoram	93.72	1	89.4	1
Nagaland	83.29	5	76.69	3
Sikkim	87.29	3	76.43	4
Tripura	92.18	2	83.15	2

Source: Census, 2011.

In Meghalaya and Nagaland females are having more literacy rate than the males' literacy rates. Arunachal stands at the bottom among the North-East states in both the gender.

Enrolment in Science Education at Higher Secondary Level

Higher secondary education is one of the most important parts of educational level which connects between the college and school, between the school education and higher education. The following table 2.3 describes the enrolment pattern among science education in North-East states in India.

Among all the North-East states Manipur has more than 70 per cents enrolment in Science education however Assam has approximately 11 per cents with the lowest enrolment in North-East states. There are big differences between Manipur and all other states in terms of Enrolment in science education at higher secondary level. States having the lowest percentage of enrolment in science education at a higher secondary level like Arunachal Pradesh and Assam has seen continuous growth in enrolment in science education. Both the states Arunachal Pradesh and Assam have seen expansion in enrolments from 19.36 per cent and 7.45 per cent in 2013-2014 to 23.63 per cent and 11.6 per cent respectively.

Table 2.3: Percentages of Enrolment in Science Subjects in Higher Secondary (2013-2014 to 2017- 2018)

States/Years	*2013-14*	*2014-15*	*2015-16*	*2016-17*	*2017-18*
ArunachalPradesh	19.36	18.03	16.95	15.9	23.63
Assam	7.45	8.39	11.81	11.74	11.6
Manipur	74.6	71.16	73.02	74.12	70.56
Meghalaya	17.47	15.72	15.95	16.77	15.83
Mizoram	22.41	20.62	17.58	18.55	18.11
Nagaland	22.73	12.97	17.55	19.21	17.84
Sikkim	25.83	20.86	21.97	22.81	22.48
Tripura	16.52	15.44	16.02	16.05	16.73

Source: U- DISE, 2014, 2015, 2016, 2017, 2018.

However, all the other states have experienced a decline in enrolment of students in science education. Manipur which stands at highest per cent of enrolment in science education has declined from 74.6 percent in 2013-2014 to 70.56 per cent in 2017-2018. Similarly, Sikkim enrolment in Sikkim has declined from 25-83 per cent in 2013-2014to 22.48 per cent in 2017- 2018. Similarly, other states like Meghalaya, Mizoram have also seen a decline in enrolment in science education. Tripura has been almost constant in science education enrolment in last five years.

Results in Science Education at Secondary Level

Enrolment is any subjects do not give the right picture of success in education at any levels. It is important to understand in terms of not only about the equality of opportunities but also equality of outcomes. The next (Table 2.4) section briefly discusses the percentage of pass students in science education at higher secondary levels for the one the year 2017-2018. The result shows an interesting finding from the U-DISE Data.

Table 2.4: Percentage of Students Passed in Science Subjects in Higher Secondary in 2017-2018

States/Category	*GENERAL*		*SC*		*ST*		*OBC*	
North-Eastern States	*Boys*	*Girls*	*Boys*	*Girls*	*Boys*	*Girls*	*Boys*	*Girls*
Arunachal Pradesh	72.46	81.43	100	50	67.84	73.9	100	100
Assam	84.54	89.25	84.22	90.24	87.92	89.02	89.12	90.01
Manipur	76.23	80.36	86.01	96.3	68.48	75.59	79.34	79.97
Meghalaya	80.9	80.82	86.67	81.82	77.79	81.97	85.71	94.12
Mizoram	39.22	13.33	100	50	82.37	85.66	75	100
Nagaland	89	98.48	91.67	95	88.85	95.03	84.78	94.74
Sikkim	82.39	95.21	94.87	90.91	92.31	92.41	86.3	92.15
Tripura	86.92	89.13	89.39	84.38	82.55	77.2	87.73	84.49

Source: U-DISE: 2017-2018.

Among the General Category students, the pass out the percentage of the Girls in science is more in the states excepts Meghalaya and Mizoram which has more pass out of the boys with comparison to girls but it is marginal difference of .08 percent in case of Meghalaya. However, in the case of Mizoram, the differences are more with gaps of more than 25 per cent in both the gender. In case of Sikkim, the pass out the percentage of girls with more than 12 percentages followed by Nagaland where pass out the percentage of girls are 10 per cent more than the boys in science education.

Coming to Scheduled Castes (SCs) students in Higher Secondary level pass of the percentage of Girls are less except Assam, Manipur and Nagaland. In Arunachal Pradesh and Mizoram, the pass out the percentage of Girls is only 50 percent however for Boys in both the states it is 100 percent. In Assam, Manipur and Nagaland the pass percentage of girls is 6 percent, 10 percent and 4 per cent more respectively in comparison to boys in the same states.

In Case of Scheduled Tribes (STs) except the Tripura the pass out the percentage of Girls are more than the boys in all the states. Among the Other Backward Classes (OBCs) pass percentage of Girls are far better than the Boys in Higher Secondary levels in science education except Tripura where the pass percentage of boys are better than the girls in science education. Overall the data shows us the girls are doing better than the boys in higher secondary schools in science education in the North-East States except minor differences.

Science Laboratory in Higher Secondary Schools

The presence of a science laboratory makes science teaching-learning interesting in schools. It increases the interest of the students in science education in general at schools levels and particularly it motivates for taking science education in higher education.

Table 2.5: Percentage of Higher Secondary Schools with Science Laboratory in 2017-2018

States/Subjects	*Physics*	*Chemistry*	*Biology*	*Mathematics*	*Computer*
ArunachalPradesh	38.51	37.27	37.89	40.37	13.04
Assam	17.24	17.46	16.78	6.91	20.42
Manipur	75.53	76.79	75.11	31.65	64.98
Meghalaya	20.35	19.76	19.47	6.19	30.09
Mizoram	17.71	17.71	14.86	1.71	13.71
Nagaland	32.79	32.24	33.88	12.57	45.36
Sikkim	52.94	50.00	51.96	21.57	72.55
Tripura	40.04	39.15	38.7	8.05	30.65

Source: U-DISE, 2018.

According to U-DISE (Table 2.5) Manipur has 75.53 per cent schools with Physics Laboratory followed by Sikkim 52.94 per cent, Tripura 40.04 per cent, Arunachal Pradesh 38.51 per cent, Nagaland 32.79 percent. Assam and Mizoram have approximately 17 per cent schools with Physics labs at higher secondary levels and Meghalaya having 20.35 per cent schools with Physics laboratory. It is interesting to understand Manipur has the highest per cent of enrolment in science education also at the higher secondary level. A similar trend can be seen in terms of Chemistry and Biology laboratory in all the states and Manipur (76.79%) occupies the top position followed by Sikkim (50%), Tripura (39.15%), Arunachal Pradesh (37.27) in availing the laboratory in Chemistry. In Biology Manipur

(75.11%), Sikkim (51.96) and Tripura (38.7%) occupy the top others are at the bottom in terms of availing the laboratory in higher secondary levels. 72.55 % of higher secondary schools are having computer laboratory in Sikkim followed by Manipur with 64.98% schools are equipped with computer laboratory. Arunachal Pradesh and Mizoram are equipped with least number of computer laboratories with 13.04 and 13.71 respectively. Except for Manipur, Sikkim and Tripura other North-East states have to improve the Laboratory in higher secondary schoolings,

Discussion and Conclusion

Education in general and science education in particular not only improves the quality of life is but also increase a person's ability to earn and participate in political and social life. Education is not only the means of development to individuals but also the overall economic development of the country and social change. Overall North-East states are better in literacy rate than the national literacy rate. Only among the north-east states, Arunachal Pradesh and Assam are lower than the national literacy rate as per the 2011 census. Similarly, in science education, only Manipur are doing much better than any other states among north-east states. Science Laboratory is available in more than 70% of higher secondary levels followed by Sikkim and Tripura in most the science disciplines in Manipur. Interestingly data shows that despite having higher literacy rates in Mizoram, enrolment data on science education at higher secondary level is not encouraging. Available of classrooms and science labs, trained teachers in science education are the important areas where states have to work upon it. As the North-East states are diverse, their enrolment in science education is also diverse. Other states in North-East can learn from Manipur in increasing their enrolment in science education at the higher secondary levels. We as a civilisation are at a crucial stage in the process of development and transformation with respect to climate change, population growth, demand for food and clean air and water. In this context the role of science is of the utmost importance. Science education must become an integral part of school education. Expansion science education enrolment requires better teachers training and supply of teachers, curriculum reforms, equal importance of theory and practice, proper funding in promoting researches.

References

Declaration, I. (2015). *Education 2030: Towards inclusive and equitable quality education and lifelong learning for all*. World Education Forum (pp. 19-22).

U-DISE, (2014), U-DISE,State Report Card, NUEPA, New Delhi.

U-DISE, (2015), U-DISE, State Report Card, NUEPA, New Delhi.

U-DISE, (2016), U-DISE, State Report Card, NUEPA, New Delhi.

U-DISE, (2017), U-DISE, State Report Card, NUEPA, New Delhi.

U-DISE, (2018), U-DISE, State Report Card, NUEPA, New Delhi.

Chapter - III

Pharmaceutical Science in North-East India: Current Status and Prospects

— Lalduhsanga Pachuau,
Mrinmoy Acharjee & Tapojyoti Das

Introduction

The word 'Pharmacy' is taken from a Greek word *Pharmakon* meaning 'drug'. Pharmacy is the art and science of preparing and dispensing medication and to provide drug- related information to the public (Fink III, 2005). Pharmacy remained an important functional part of medicine for a long time. However, with increasing variety of available drugs and the complexity of their preparation, a devoted professional specialized in the art and science of drug preparations became a necessity. As a result, Pharmacy was officially separated from medicine for the first time in 1240 AD by Emperor Frederick II of Germany who regulated the practice of pharmacy within the part of his kingdom called the Two Sicilies (Allen Jr., Popovich and Ansel, 2011). Such a separation indicates that the pharmacy profession required special knowledge and skills to provide proper medical care to the people. Therefore, proper training and education is highly important in providing the right kind of education to the budding pharmacists. Knowing this importance, the Government of India enacted the *Pharmacy Act* in 1948 to control the profession of pharmacy and its education. Pharmacy Council of India (PCI) established as per the Pharmacy Act 1948 and the All India Council for Technical Education (AICTE) became the two statutory bodies that regulate pharmacy education in India.

Pharmacy education in India can be traced back to the introduction of certificate level course in pharmacy by the Portuguese in 1842 at Goa

(PCI & IPA, 2009). A 3-years Bachelor degree (B.Pharm.) course was initiated in India by Banaras Hindu University (BHU), Varanasi in 1937 and prior to Indian independence in 1947, there were three institutions offering B.Pharm. course in India at BHU Varanasi, Punjab University and LM College of Pharmacy Ahmedabad (Basak and Sathyanarayana, 2010). With the passing of the Pharmacy Act that prescribes minimum qualification for the practice of pharmacy in India, several institutions and Universities across the country started to offer courses in pharmacy ranging from Diploma to Doctor of Pharmacy, and the numbers have greatly increased in the last few decades (PCI & IPA, 2009).

According to AICTE, in 2018-2019 sessions, there are 1210 Pharmacy colleges in India approved by AICTE to conduct UG course in Pharmacy, out of these only 9 Colleges are from North East India (NEI). There are only 5 Colleges/University Departments approved by AICTE to conduct M.Pharm. course in NEI. A recent report of the North Eastern Development Finance Corporation Ltd (NEDFi) released states that North-Eastern states needed to improve their teaching and learning of science and mathematics in schools (NEDFi, 2017). In general, this is also true for higher and technical education as well. Pharmacy education in the NEI begins with the setting up of the first Diploma in Pharmacy (D.Pharm.) course in 1962 at the Institute of Pharmacy, Assam Medical College, Dibrugarh. Since then, the development in Pharmacy education has been gradual. To our knowledge, detail and proper study on the history and development of Pharmacy education in NEI has not been reported. Therefore, current study has been conducted to reflect the current status of Pharmacy education in NEI region and to provide a possible future direction in this area of education to the policy makers.

Materials and Methods

In the current study, we analyze the data available from both AICTE and PCI websites. Information is also collected from websites of Colleges/ Universities in NEI offering courses in Pharmacy. Interviews are also conducted with senior professors who are teaching pharmacy in NEI for decades

Results and Discussion

Pharmacy education in the NEI begins with the setting up of the first Diploma in Pharmacy (D.Pharm.) course in 1962 at the Institute of Pharmacy, Assam Medical College, Dibrugarh. Under graduate (B.Pharm.)

and Post graduate (M.Pharm.) courses in Pharmacy at the Northeast regional level also initiated from Dibrugarh University in 1983 and 2002 respectively. Currently, there are 9 institutions offering AICTE approved B.Pharm. course in the Northeast and 7 institutions are approved by PCI for conducting B.Pharm. course (AICTE, 2018; PCI, 2018). There are only five institutions offering PG course in Pharmacy in the entire Northeast. Out of the 9 Central Universities in Northeast India, only 1 (Tripura University) is offering PG course in its University Campus, and two others (Mizoram University and Sikkim University) are offering it through its affiliated Colleges. Department of Pharmaceutical Science, Dibrugarh University is the only institution with NIRF Ranking (22nd rank) in Pharmacy from the entire Northeast India region.

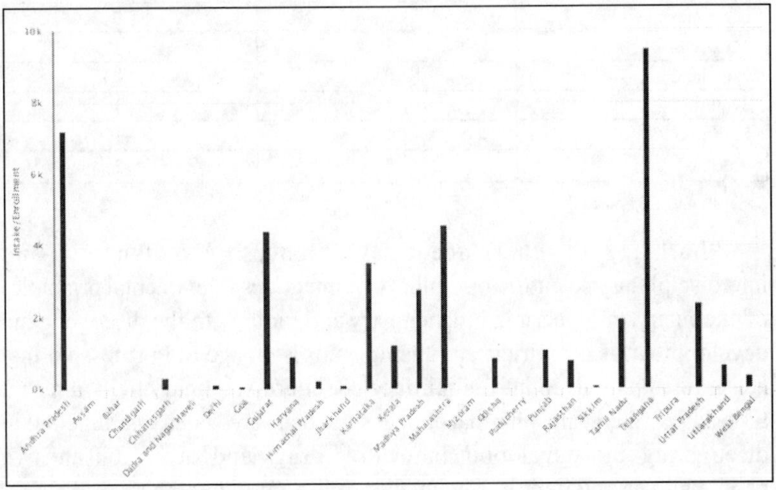

Source: AICTE.

Fig. 3.1: State-Wise Distribution of Students Enrolled for M.Pharm. (2017-2018)

As per the latest statistics available from the websites of AICTE and Pharmacy Council of India, the yearly enrollment of UG course in Pharmacy (B.Pharm.) at the institutions in Northeast India is totaled at 408 while the total enrollment capacity from the same region in PG courses is only 175. This indicates that every year more than 230 B.Pharm. graduates from the entire NER are either denied of their dream of securing a seat in PG courses or have to move to other parts of the country to pursue their dream which comes with a certain payments which many deserving candidates could not afford to do so. There are no UG/PG Pharmacy institutions located in states such as Arunachal Pradesh, Manipur, Meghalaya and Nagaland, while in states like Maharashtra alone, there are 233 AICTE approved institutions offering B.Pharm. course. Considering the 2011 Census, about 5 lakhs people in Maharashtra share the services of one AICTE approved pharmacy college, while in NEI more than 50 lakhs people share the service of one such approved Pharmacy College.

Table 3.1: Number of Institutes from NER offering AICTE or PCI Approved Course in Pharmacy

States	*No. of Institutes offering UG course in Pharmacy*	*No. of Institutes offering PG course in Pharmacy*
Arunachal Pradesh	0	0
Assam	4	2
Manipur	0	0
Meghalaya	0	0
Mizoram	1	1
Nagaland	0	0
Tripura	1	1
Sikkim	1	1
Total	**7**	**5**

Source: AICTE and PCI.

Pharmacy or Pharmaceutical Sciences is a dynamic and interdisciplinary scientific discipline that integrates fundamental principles of chemistry, engineering, biochemistry and biology to the discovery and development of new drugs and therapies. It is an age old profession that has gradually evolved into a multifaceted, interdisciplinary field in recent times. Over the years, pharmaceutical scientists have been instrumental in discovering and developing innovative drugs and save thousands of people's lives and improve the quality of life for many others.

Pharmaceutical industry in India is one of the largest and most advanced among the developing countries. In terms of value, the Indian pharmaceutical industry ranks globally as the 14th largest market by sales value and globally ranked 3rd by volumes of sales. India is also among the top five manufacturers of bulk drugs in the world (PCI & IPA, 2009). As a result, about 70% of the country's demand for medicine is met by the Indian pharmaceutical industry. Apart from this, India is also holding the record of the highest number of United States FDA approved manufacturing units outside the United States. Today, there are 270 large R & D based pharmaceutical companies and 5600 smaller licensed manufacturers in India. Ergo, these industries provides plethora of employment opportunities

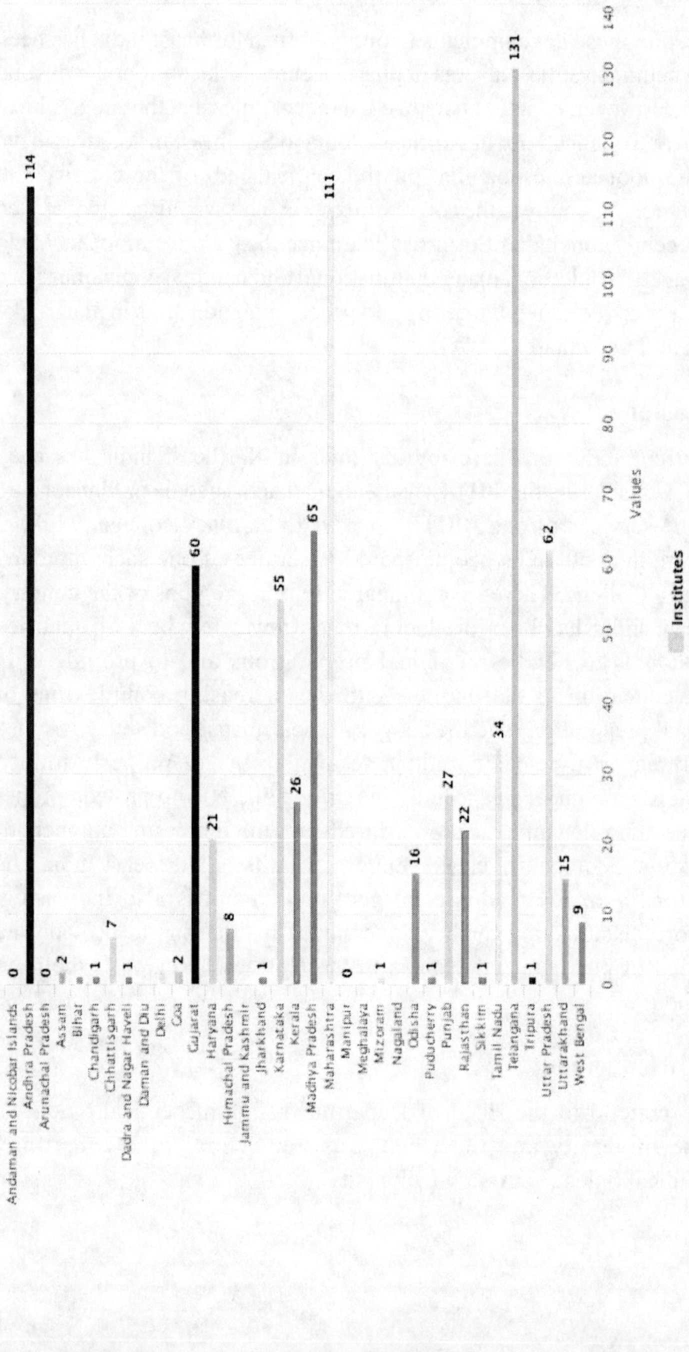

Source: AICTE

Fig. 3.2: State-Wise Distribution of Pharmacy Institutes (PG in Pharmacy) in India

to the young graduates in Pharmacy. Barring these, the pharmacy graduates also have multitudes of scopes in the area of Research and Development, Academics, Regulatory, Pharmacy Practice and Clinical Research.

Despite these developments in our country, Northeast India has been lagging behind in almost all area of pharmaceutical education and industrial settings. However, it has been realized in recent times that the geographical location and connectivity of Northeast India to South Asian countries have open the door as the potential pharmaceutical hub of the country and contribute significantly to the country's exports. This was also demonstrated in the recently concluded Northeast Pharmaceutical Convention 2017 held at Guwahati. In addition, many multinational and national companies have already set up their manufacturing and processing industries in places like Sikkim and Guwahati.

Conclusion

The current status of Pharmacy institutes in Northeast India has been studied. Considering the 2011 Census, about 5 lakhs people in Maharashtra share the services of one AICTE approved pharmacy college, while in NEI more than 50 lakhs people share the service of one such approved Pharmacy College. Therefore, compared to other regions of the country, Northeast India has been producing much fewer numbers of qualified professionals to handle medicinal preparations and to provide drug related education to the public. With the increasing complexities of medicinal preparations and the danger of their misuse and abuse posing a grave threat to the society, adequate availability of properly trained Pharmacists are needed especially in regions like NEI to provide proper guidance and relevant education. Moreover, with increasing numbers of multinational companies establishing their units in Northeast India, the scope for pharmacy graduates to get employment is also increasing. Therefore, establishing quality educational institutions to provide the right kind of pharmacy educations in the Northeast Region is the need of the hour.

Acknowledgement

We are grateful to the Head of Department, Pharmaceutical Sciences, Assam University and the Dean, Susruta School of Medical and Paramedical Sciences, Assam University.

References

AICTE (2018). https://www.aicte-india.org (last accessed on 31st October, 2018).

Allen Jr, L.V., Popovich, N.G., Ansel, H.C. (2011). Introduction to drugs and pharmacy. In, *Ansel's Pharmaceutical Dosage forms and Drug Delivery Systems* (9th Ed., pp. 1-25). Baltimore, Maryland: Lippincott Williams & Wilkins.

Basak, S.C., Sathyanarayana, D. (2010). Pharmacy education in India. *American Journal of Pharmaceutical Education 74*(4), Article 68.

Fink II, J.L. (2005). Scope of Pharmacy, In R. Hendrickson (Ed.), *Remington: The science and practice of pharmacy* (pp. 3). Baltimore, Maryland: Lippincott Williams & Wilkins.

PCI (2018). www.pci.nic.in (last accessed on 31st October, 2018)

Pharmacy Council of India (PCI), Indian Pharmaceutical Association (IPA). (2009). A Career in Pharmacy. Mumbai, IPA.

NEDFi (2017). Study Report: Regional Plan and Status of Science Education in Schools in North Eastern Region (NER).

Chapter - IV

Gender and Academic Career in Science: An Explorative Study in Universities of North-Eastern States of India

— *Nithiya Amirtham S*

Introduction

Gender inequalities in education and work force in India have been a concern for the government and its agencies. Several commissions and committees have been formed to understand the gender inequality in education. The reports of these committees and commissions mention about various suggestions for improvement (see for the policy reports, Sharma and Mazumdar, 2012) including the committee on the status of women in India (Committee on the Status of Women in India, 1974). Cultural and societal norms show significant influence on women's decision in choice of work and mobility in India (Chaudhary and Verick, 2014). The variation in socio-cultural fabric among the states and regions of India too could contribute to differences in perspectives towards gender in education and work force participation. Even among north-eastern states existence of heterogeneous social structure is observed (Biswas, 2008). Gender discrimination in a society is related to the status of women in India (Sinha, 2015). Study shows regional and institutional variations in perceptions towards women in science. The study further reported that in eastern regional institutes of India, the attitude towards women are respectful and higher education is seen as desirable for women but in the northern region conservatism prevails in the society towards women (Gupta and Sharma,

2003). Northern part of India showed patriarchal mindset and low social status of women while the south showed more favourable gender relations and high social status of women (Dyson and Moore, 1983). High status of women in the south and east are linked with economic role of women in agriculture in those days (Bardhan, 1974) and it is extended to the north-east of India on the high status enjoyed by women of this region traditionally (Sinha, 2015).

The study focuses on understanding the gender inequality in sciences in north-east region of India. Although the study includes universities located in north-eastern states of India, analysing gender representation in culturally bound manner is not possible as the faculty working in these central universities is from across the country having diverse socio-cultural backgrounds. This study will provide only a picture of extant gender representation in universities in north-eastern states. Socio-cultural perspectives are discussed in general and it is not specific to region/states.

The objectives of this study include (i) to find out the gender representation in faculty in-position in science disciplines at higher education level in north-eastern states of India; (ii) to identify the differences between physical and biological sciences in gender representation of faculty in-position at higher education level in north-eastern states of India.

Socio-Cultural Matrix of Gender and Science Career

Gender representation in science career is a global concern and various studies across the world have been conducted to understand the phenomena. Policy initiatives on reducing gender gap have been successful in many countries. Study conducted in Netherland showed leaky pipeline exists in academia especially at top level of career in Science, Technology, Engineering and Mathematics (STEM). The decline in number of women was seen from doctoral programmes. Due to policy practices, improvement in gender representation is observed (Herschberg and Berger, 2015). Gender disparity is observed in STEM employment in Australia (Healy, Mavromaras, and Zhu, 2013). It is said that balancing work and family demand seen problematic for women. Stereotypes and social factors regarding gender and STEM disciplines exist in Australia (Roberts, 2014). Participation of women in STEM fields in Japan is relatively lower than western countries and Australia. Several initiatives including child care facilities, career counseling, and incentives for employees etc. have been taken to improve women's participation in workforce in Japan (Ishikawa and Moehle, 2013). Underrepresentation of women in STEM higher education and workforce in United States is a continuing phenomenon (Turner and Bowen, 1999; Fox, 2001; Mullen, 2010); only less than 30% women are holding STEM jobs (National Science Foundation, 2015). Enrolment of male in STEM fields in higher education was more in Turkey, but the trend has seen a considerable changes in reduction of gender gap between males and females between 2002 and 2012 (Korkut-Owen et al., 2014). Underrepresentation is seen in socioeconomically disadvantaged individuals in STEM fields in Turkey (Shaw and Barbuti, 2010).

Indian scenario of gender and STEM career are not an exception from the above mentioned countries in the world. Besides, the socio-cultural and economical condition of the Indian society makes more complications in women's education and career in general and STEM education in particular. Historically women's academic career is restricted by discrimination, cultural constraints in India (Thelwall et al., 2019) and cultural expectations (Chandrakar, 2014). Visibility of women is linked to constructions of passivity while men's visibility is linked to centers of power which impact procedures of appointment, promotion and governance in Indian universities (Chanana, 2003). It can be said that gender issues in India are different from better researched countries like United States as influence of family in women's decisions and the economical condition of the country (Vindhya, 2007). Research conducted by (INSA, 2004) shows that women are prevented in choosing science and technology courses, in that too specifically physical sciences and mathematics which are considered suitable for male, due to the conventional mindset internalised and passed over generations. Women scientists and engineers employed as faculty are very few in academic institutes of higher learning in India and they encounter difficulties at work due to their gender which is connected with the existing patrifocal ideology at workplace (Gupta and Sharma, 2002). Career paths of women are seen flatter than men and it is shown that disparity in academic rank prevails despite considering differential productivity (Kumar, 2001). Women professionals in India reported that family responsibility affects career decisions (Buddhapriya, 2009), particularly, lack of support in child care is one of leading causes of post Ph.D. underrepresentation of women in academic career in India (Godbole and Ramaswamy, 2008). It is also observed that the complexities involved in women's underrepresentation in science in India is not well studied (Gupta, 2015). Hence this study will help in understanding the representation of women in science in India.

Methodology

Purposive sampling technique is applied in selection of sample. In north-eastern region of India, all the eight sister states which includes Assam, Arunachal Pradesh, Manipur, Meghalaya, Mizoram, Nagaland, Sikkim and Tripura are considered for the study. The population of the study is faculty working in physics, chemistry, botany and zoology departments of universities in north-east India. All the central universities located in each states of north-east India form the sample of the study. Assam has two central universities and other states have one each. In Assam, Botany and Zoology disciplines are not offered as separate subjects in any central universities, rather it is offered as life sciences and bioinformatics in one university and in another university only applied biological sciences subjects are offered. In this study for Assam state, only one university details are taken under biological sciences i.e., life sciences and bioinformatics discipline. Faculty details of each required departments in this study are taken from the respective university websites. Only permanent/regular faculties of the departments are included in the study. All these faculties are involved in teaching and research in their respective disciplines in sciences. The study assumes that, all universities are updating their faculty details in the websites whenever new faculties join the department. The calculated values in this study are based on the information given in department websites regarding the number of regular faculties (as of May 2020).

Results

Table 4.1: Average Gender Representation of Faculty in Science Disciplines in Higher Education in North-East India

States	*Male (%)*	*Female (%)*
Assam	81.22	18.78
Arunachal Pradesh	93.75	06.25
Manipur	68.75	31.25
Meghalaya	79.51	20.49
Mizoram	84.52	15.48
Nagaland	83.73	16.27
Sikkim	86.01	13.99
Tripura	95.00	05.00

Calculated Values.

The findings show that female representation in faculty position in science disciplines in all north-eastern states is lower than male. Among the eight states, Manipur shows better representation of female faculty (31.25%) in science disciplines and is higher education among north-eastern states whereas, the Tripura shows the lowest (5%) followed by the Arunachal Pradesh (6.25%).The female representation in other states are staying between 10 and 20 percent. Overall female are underrepresented in science disciplines in higher education in all the north-eastern states of India. (Table 4.1)

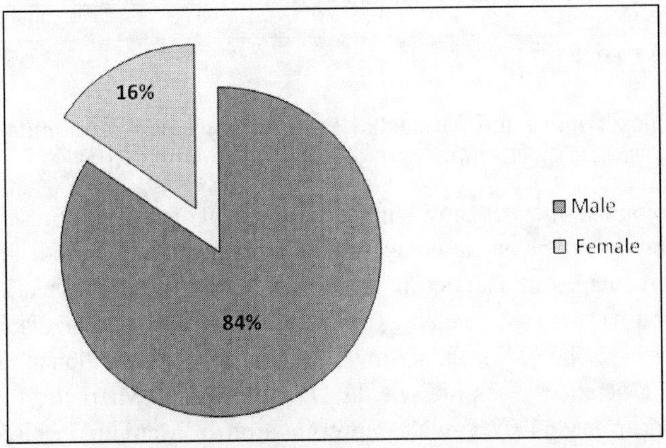

Fig. 4.1: Gender Representation of Faculties in Science Disciplines in Higher Education in North-Eastern States of India

The average percentages of gender representation in faculties of science disciplines in north-east India shows 84% male and 16% female in position. It shows that male representation is higher in sciences than female in higher education in north-east India. (Fig 4.1)

The findings of the average number of gender representation in physical sciences disciplines in higher education in north-eastern states of India show that, there is no female faculty in Arunachal Pradesh and Tripura in the selected disciplines of physical sciences category. Meghalaya shows 6.25% and Sikkim shows 8.33% of female faculty in physical sciences. Manipur shows better representation of female faculty in physical sciences having 25% and Nagaland has 21.43% of female representation. The remaining states have percentage values between 15% and 20%. The findings show that there is underrepresentation of females in science disciplines in faculty representation however in physical sciences

Table 4.2: Average Gender Representation of Faculty in Physical and Biological Sciences Disciplines in Higher Education in North-East India

States	*Physical Sciences*		*Biological Sciences*	
	Male (%)	*Female (%)*	*Male (%)*	*Female (%)*
Assam	83.35	16.65	76.92	23.08
Arunachal Pradesh	100	0	87.50	12.50
Manipur	75.00	25.00	62.50	37.50
Meghalaya	93.75	6.25	65.28	34.72
Mizoram	84.52	15.48	84.52	15.48
Nagaland	78.57	21.43	88.89	11.11
Sikkim	91.67	8.33	80.36	19.64
Tripura	100	0	90.00	10.00

* *Calculated Values.*

disciplines Tripura and Arunachal Pradesh have zero representation in north-eastern states of India in physical science. (Table 4.2)

Biological sciences show slight improvement of faculty representation comparatively to physical sciences in higher education in north-east India. Few percentages of female are visible in Arunachal Pradesh (12.50%) and Tripura (10%) where there is no female faculty in selected disciplines of physical sciences. Nagaland shows less female representation in selected biological sciences disciplines i.e. 11.11% followed by Mizoram (15.48%) and Sikkim (19.64%). Female representation in Manipur in biological sciences disciplines is higher among all other north-eastern states of India. Manipur shows 37.50% female faculties in selected biological sciences

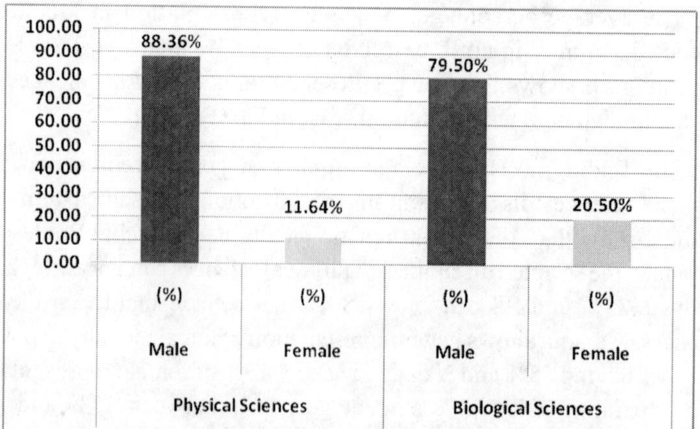

Fig. 4.2: Differences between Gender in Physical and Biological Sciences in Faculties in-position in Higher Education in North-Eastern States of India

disciplines in this study which is followed by Meghalaya (34.72%) and Assam (23.08%). Despite of having better representation of females in biological sciences, they are still underrepresented in all the north-eastern states of India. (Table 4.2)

The overall gender representation in physical and biological sciences in selected disciplines of faculties in higher education in north-east India shows variations between the physical and biological sciences. In physical sciences, representation of male is higher (88.36%) where only 11.64% female are found in faculty in position. Rather in biological sciences, despite having lower percentage of female (20.50%), comparatively to physical sciences it is higher. In both physical and biological sciences categories, the percentage of female faculty in-position is highly underrepresented in higher education in north-east India. (Fig. 4.2)

Discussion

There is general stereotypical belief in India that women are suitable for teaching profession however the results are contradictory for the same in higher education. The gender disparity in academic career in science disciplines in higher education indicates that, higher the level of position in academics, lower the number of women in the position. It means that females are underrepresented in higher level of academic career that are considered as prestigious and possessing decision making roles. All India survey on higher education data shows that women are outnumbered than men until M.Phil level in higher education and even in doctoral research, representation of women is better (MHRD, 2019) however not satisfactory. After the doctoral degree there is drastic decline in number of women in academic career in science disciplines and women are mostly underrepresented in it. Several studies find that the impact of the regional, social and cultural characteristics on gender plays vital role in the underrepresentation of women in entering into science. The current study also tries to understand the underrepresentation of women in universities located in northeastern part of India, which is considered as socially and culturally distinct and regionally different. The selected universities in this study are central government institutions and have equal opportunities to all candidates appear for interviews and hence recruited from across the country. It is important to clarify that the purpose of the study is limited to see the representation of women in selected disciplines in universities located in north-eastern states of India. The purpose of the study is also not to generalize the result for the larger level.

Physical sciences are considered as lucrative subjects than biological sciences. Slightly higher number of women is seen in biological sciences than in physical sciences. This is seen as a continuation of women enrolled in higher education courses in science disciplines in India. As per AISHE (2019) data, the enrolment of women in Ph.D. has reached to the following percentages: - physics- 39%; chemistry- 43%; botany-59%; and zoology-57%. Proportion of women is higher than men in life sciences than physical sciences (UNESCO, 2010; Webb et al., 2002). The representation of women in doctoral higher education in physical sciences is not equal to men. Similar phenomena is observed among Dutch higher education where women are majority from bachelors to masters and from doctoral research onwards the number gradually decreases and ends up with lowest number at full professor grade (Herschberg and Berger, 2015). But in biological sciences category women are enrolled more than men in India. It is a continuity of past years' trend in these four science disciplines. Despite having more women than men in biological sciences, the steep decrease in number of women in science academic career requires further in-depth analysis. It is important to emphasise that educational attainment of women is not translated into scientific career attainment and also in advancement in rank in comparison with men (Sonnert and Holton, 1995a, 1995b). This needs analysis in socio-cultural perspectives as socio-cultural factors push women out of STEM pipeline in India (Kumar, 2009).

In north-eastern states of India, most of the selected universities in this study are located in remote places. Travelling to these locations is not as smooth as like plain regions as majority of them are located on hills. Familial influence in sending women to remote places for career hinders women's career choices in general and science disciplines in particular as science requires lots time to be spent in the laboratory even in late hours. Research shows that barriers of women in science and engineering disciplines in India include families' concern on travelling alone, odd working hours, long period of study and fear of failing to get suitable match (Mukhopadhyay 1994); is still seen relevant. Besides, there is lack of infrastructural facilities in-terms of quarters for faculty, crèches and schools for children inside the campus and non-availability of low cost local transportation facilities in the locality become impediment in choosing career in north-east India. Due to lack of crèche facilities women in India delays entry into workforce and research in higher levels of education (Gupta and Sharma, 2013) and it should be analysed in connection with low representation of women in higher education. Survey conducted by ministry of program implementation shows that females spend double of the time in taking care of children, sick and elder person in India than men (Government of India, 2000). Women are under dual work role burden, men have minimal or no involvement in home and family related burden, brings convenience for men to move anywhere easily for career. Study shows that 26.2% of women to 1 male experienced disturbance in career due to domestic and marriage related reasons as university teaching jobs are immovable in India and is seen as constraint in women's academic career (Chanana, 2003). The development efforts taken by India since last sixty years have not shown major transformation in position of women in socio-cultural domain (Sinha, 2015).

Women centric policies and positive discrimination strategies to improve representation of women in academics and workforce participation especially in STEM disciplines are essential for India. Attracting women to science, supporting women already in science or changing science to be more inclusive of women are some of the initiatives required in sciences for women (Cronin and Roger, 1999). Providing exposure to own gender role models is viewed as essential for reducing gender gap in STEM (Blickenstaff, 2005; Asgari and Dasgupta, 2010; Richman, van Dellen, and Wood, 2011). Positive discrimination policies have proven record of reduced gender gap in Turkish higher education enrolment in STEM fields (Çalýk, Ültay, Kolomuç, and Aytar, 2015). Providing category wise women reservation at entry level of academic career and in promotion, reservation for women in project allotments, relaxation in leave polices for women and extra incentives for women working in institutions located at remote and difficult terrains would bring changes in representation of women and their utilisation of talents and knowledge in higher education. In addition to that, improving infrastructural facilities in higher educational institutions to reduce the difficulties and challenges of women will bring visible changes in the percentage of women representation in academic career in India.

Conclusion

The current study reveals that there is stark underrepresentation of women in selected disciplines in universities located in north-eastern states of India. Among all the north-eastern states of India, Manipur shows better results in female representation and Tripura shows the lowest number of female representation in selected disciplines. Overall results based on physical and biological sciences category of disciplines show clear underrepresentation of women in these disciplines. In physical sciences, Arunachal Pradesh and Tripura show no female representation in faculty in-position in sciences in selected higher education institutions. Between these subject categories, female representation is slightly higher or equal in biological sciences comparatively with physical sciences except Nagaland. Despite of better representation of females in M.Phil and Ph.D. in higher education, women's representation decreases in science disciplines in academic career. It can be understood from the present study that the leaky pipeline pushes women from academic career involving science disciplines due to the influence of existing socio-cultural factors in Indian society. Reducing the challenges of women at academic career would bring greater changes in participation at workforce level and in growth and development of country.

References

Asgari, S., Dasgupta, N., and Cote, N. G. (2010). When does contact with successful ingroup members change self-stereotypes?. *Social Psychology,41*(3), 203-211.

Bardhan, P. K. (1974). On life and death questions. *Economic and Political Weekly*, *9*(32/33), 1293-1304.

Biswas, N. B. (2008). *Education in North-East India*. Delhi: Shipra.

Blickenstaff, J.C. (2005). Women and science careers: leaky pipeline or gender filter?. *Gender and education*, *17*(4), 369-386.

Buddhapriya, S. (2009). Work-family challenges and their impact on career decisions: A study of Indian women professionals. *Vikalpa*, *34*(1), 31-46.

Çalýk, M., Ültay, N., Kolomuç, A., and Aytar, A. (2015). A cross-age study of science student teachers' chemistry attitudes. *Chemistry Education Research and Practice*, *16*(2), 228-236.

Chanana, K. (2003). Visibility, gender, and the careers of women faculty in an Indian university. *McGill Journal of Education, 38*(003).

Chandrakar, C. L. (2014). Why "Ritiya" could not go to sell vegetables? Myth versus reality in terms of caste, culture and livelihood. *Journal of Rural Social Sciences, 29*(2), 48-56.

Chaudhary, R., and Verick, S. (2014). *Female labour force participation in India and beyond*. New Delhi: ILO.

Committee on the Status of Women in India. (1974). *Towards Equality: Report of the Committee on the Status of Women in India*. Government of India, Department of Social Welfare, Ministry of Education and Social Welfare.

Cronin, C. and Roger, A. (1999). Theorizing progress: women in science, engineering, and technology in higher education. *Journal of Research in Science Teaching, 36*(6), 639–661.

Dyson, T., and Moore, M. (1983). On kinship structure, female autonomy, and demographic behavior in India. *Population and development review*, *9*(1), 35-60.

Fox, M.F. (2001). Women, science, and academia: Graduate education and careers, *Gender Society*, *15* (5), 654–666.

Godbole, R., and Ramaswamy, R. (2008). Women scientists in India. *Women in science and technology in Asia. KAST: Gyeonggi-Do, Republic of Korea*, 67-84.

Government of India. (2000). Government of India, *The Time Use Survey* (New Delhi: Ministry of Statistics and Programme Implementation).

Gupta, N. (2015). Gender equality in science in India: an undeveloped agenda. *Current Science*, *109*(1), 9-10.

Gupta, N. and Sharma, A.K. (2003). Patrifocal concerns in the lives of women in academic science: Continuity of tradition and emerging challenges. *Indian Journal of Gender Studies, 10*(2), 279-305.

Gupta, N., and Sharma, A. K. (2002). Women academic scientists in India. *Social studies of science*, *32*(5-6), 901-915.

Healy, J., Mavromaras, K. and Zhu, R. (2013). *The STEM labour market in Australia.* Contributing consultant report to 'STEM: Country Comparisons' project. National Institute of Labour Studies, Flinders University, on behalf of ACOLA. Australian Office for the Chief Scientist: Canberra. Retrieved from https://acola.org/wp-content/uploads/2018/12/Consultant-Report-Australian-Labour-Market.pdf

Herschberg, C., Berger, L.J. (2015). *Academic careers and gender inequality: Leaky pipeline and interrelated phenomena in seven European countries.* Trendo: University of Trento. Retrieved from https://hdl.handle.net/2066/181846

INSA. (2004). Science career for Indian women: *An examination of Indian women's access to and retention in scientific careers*. Indian National Science Academy: New Delhi.

Ishikawa, M. and Moehle, A. (2013). *STEM Country Comparisons: Japan*. Contributing consultant report to 'STEM: Country Comparisons' project. On behalf of ACOLA, for the Australian Office for the Chief Scientist: Canberra. Retrieved from https://acola.org/wp-content/uploads/2018/12/Consultant-Report-Japan.pdf

Kumar, N. (2009). *Women and Science in India – A Reader*, Oxford University Press.

Kumar, N. (2001). Gender and stratification in science: An empirical study in the Indian setting. *Indian journal of gender studies*, *8*(1), 51-67.

MHRD (2019). *All India Survey on Higher Education (2018-19)*. Retrieved from http://aishe.nic.in/aishe/viewDocument.action?documentId=262

Mukhopadhyay, C. C. (1994). Family structure and Indian women's participation in science and engineering. *Women, education and family structure in India*, 103-132.

Mullen, A.L. (2010). *Degrees of Inequality: Culture, Class and Gender in American Higher Education*, Baltimore, MD: Johns Hopkins University Press.

National Science Foundation. (2015). Report on women, minorities, and persons with disabilities in science and engineering. Retrieved from https://www.nsf.gov/statistics/2015/nsf15311 /start.cfm.

Owen, F. K., Kelecioðlu, H., and Owen, D. W. (2014). A decade of change gender trends in university enrollment: Implications for career counseling. *Journal of Human Sciences*, *11*(1), 794-813.

Richman, L. S., van Dellen, M. R., and Wood, W. (2011). How women cope: Being a numerical minority in a male-dominated profession. *Journal of Social Issues, 67*, 492–509.

Roberts, K. (2014). Engaging more women and girls in mathematics and STEM fields: The international evidence. *Recuperado de http://amsi. org. au/publications/ gender-report-*20104.

Sharma, K. (2011). *Changing the terms of the discourse: Gender, equality and the Indian state*. Pearson India.

Shaw, E. J., and Barbuti, S. (2010). Patterns of persistence in intended college major with a focus on STEM majors. *NACADA Journal*, *30*(2), 19-34.

Sinha, A. (2015). Gender bias in India's north-eastern region: its manifestations, causes and consequences. *Journal of North East India Studies*, *5*, (1), 12-29.

Sonnert, G. and Holton, G. (1995a). *Gender differences in science careers: the project access Study* (New Brunswick, NJ, Rutgers University Press).

Sonnert, G. and Holton, G. (1995b). *Who succeeds in science?* (New Brunswick, NJ, Rutgers University Press).

Thelwall, M., Bailey, C., Makita, M., Sud, P., and Madalli, D. P. (2019). Gender and research publishing in India: Uniformly high inequality?. *Journal of Informetrics*, *13*(1), 118-131.

UNESCO Institute for Statistics (Ed.). (2010). *Global education digest* 2010: *comparing education statistics across the world*. UNESCO Institute for Statistics: UNESCO.

Vindhya, U. (2007). Quality of women's lives in India: Some findings from two decades of psychological research on gender. *Feminism & Psychology, 17*(3), 337-356.

Webb, R. M., Lubinski, D., and Benbow, C. P. (2002). Mathematically facile adolescents with math-science aspirations: New perspectives on their educational and vocational development. *Journal of Educational Psychology*, *94*(4), 785.

Chapter - V

Rural Students and Science Education in Higher Education in Meghalaya: Problems and Challenges

— Ferrando Lyngdoh Nonglait &
Euodia B. Myrthong

Introduction

Education is a major component of human capital. It plays an important role in fostering economic growth and enriching the overall quality of life and it is necessary for the growth and development of any community. In the modern age, the importance of education has been realized by almost all the people in the world. Even people in remote areas have realized the value of education related to their daily activities. Moreover, today, we are living in a society where science plays a very important role in every sphere of our life and science education is very important for the development of any country. The growth of our country depends on the quality of science education. Thus, science education should not be limited only to the urban areas and among those who are from an economically well but it should spread its wings towards the rural areas and to those who are economically challenged. People in the rural areas are not restrained from the influence of technology in their day-to- day life, but what they need is an opportunity of how to develop their scientific knowledge so that they can use the available resources around them judiciously. In fact science education is the basis and foundation for establishing a well developed and systematized society.

Review of Related Literature and Rationale of the Study

Solutions based on science are more likely to provide remedial measures to most problems that our country faced, and yet science education as we understand today, is not available to a vast human population (Kaptan &Timurlenk, 2012). Rural Students were found to be at a disadvantage at the higher education level, especially when it comes to science education. Studies conducted showed that Rural Students were less likely to take up science education at the higher level as most of them have a poor foundation in Mathematics, Science and English right from the Primary level (Thyrniang, 1st July 2013). Further, the severe shortage of science and mathematics teachers at the primary and secondary level in the state is an obstacle for rural students to pursue higher education. Moreover, in many schools in rural areas, there are no qualified sciences and mathematics teachers at the primary, upper primary and secondary levels (Thyrniang, 7th April 2016) and this prevents rural students to take up science education at the higher level. Rural Students faced the lack of colleges offering science education in the rural areas and most of the college offering science education are located in the state capital Shillong, as according to Dash & Mawthoh (2010) less finance is needed to start the Arts colleges and more finance is needed to start the science colleges besides laboratories, equipment,and other facilities are needed to start them. This regional imbalance in the higher education sector in the state has led to a wide-scale migration of students from rural to urban areas as well as high drop-out rate (The Shillong Times, 11 July 2017). Rural Students who migrate from rural to urban areas for a better education also often face problems such as a lack of decent accommodations (UN Administrator, 2013) and not having the family' daily supports (Pheko et al., 2014).Rural students also faced a lot of difficulties while writing and speaking English language and as a result face difficulty in communicating with teachers and other pupils in higher education (Dwivedi & Chakravarty, 2015). The lack of knowledge about courses, institutes, scholarships, and the future prospect is a major factor Rural Students in India are least likely to go to college (Akhtar, 2013). Moreover, it was observed that schools in the rural areas are invariably of poor quality and which lack basic facilities for science education. It was also observed that Rural Students in Meghalaya usually have parents who are illiterate and lack awareness about science education and hence cannot guide their children as educated parents do. Further, many Rural Students also don't have college educated role-model to encourage them to pursue higher education in the science streams as students from the rural areas generally opt for arts education. Given that no studies have been found so far on the problems and challenges of Rural Students in science education in Meghalaya. Thus, there is a need to study the same as it will contribute to the existing body of knowledge in the field of education and for the improvement of the status of Rural Students in science education for their quality development.

Statement of the Problem

Science education provides benefits to each community in which students live and work. Since this study attempt to explore the problems and challenges faced by Rural Students in science education in higher education. The study is therefore entitled as, 'Rural Students and Science Education in Higher Education: Problems and Challenges'.

Operational Definition of the Terms Used

The operational definitions of the terms used are as follows:

1. *Problems*: Problems in this study refers to those situations which hinder the progress of Rural Students in higher education. These include the psychological aspect of the individual, their socio-cultural background, the economic status, quality of the available physical infrastructure and quality of teachers.
2. *Challenges*: Challenges refers to new and difficult tasks encountered by Rural Students to deal with such as the transition from school to college, migration and adjusting to new places and teachers, language and communication.
3. *Rural Students:* Rural Students refers to all students coming from all areas other than urban areas as described in the Census of India, 2011. This implies that Rural Students are all those students who do not come from those places which fall under a Municipality, Corporation or Cantonment or Notified Town Area, or those places with a minimum population of 5,000 or those places at least 75% of the male working population was non-agricultural and/or those places with a density population of at least 400 sq. Km. (i.e. 1000 per sq. Mile).
4. *Higher Education:* Higher education in this study refers to the education in the collegiate level, after the +2 stage of schooling.

Objectives of the Study

The objectives of the study are as follows:

1. To study the problems faced by rural students in science education.
2. To study the challenges faced by rural students in science education.

Research Questions

1. What are the problems faced by rural students in science education?
2. What are the challenges faced by rural students in science education?

Delimitation of the Study

The study was delimited to the Rural Students of Meghalaya studying in 1st and 3rd semester's courses in the Science stream in the general colleges affiliated to North-Eastern Hill University. It will also be delimited to one district that is East Khasi Hills District of Meghalaya.

Methodology of the Study

(a) **Method:** The present study was carried out through the use of the descriptive survey method.

(b) **Population:** The population of the study includes all the 1st and 3rd semester Rural Students of Meghalaya studying in the Science streams in the colleges affiliated to North-Eastern Hill University located in East Khasi Hills District of Meghalaya. To identify the 1st and 3rd semester Rural Students of Meghalaya studying in the Science streams in the colleges affiliated to North-Eastern Hill University located in East Khasi Hills District of Meghalaya the investigator has went to all the general colleges affiliated to North-Eastern Hill University which are located in East Khasi Hills District and sought the help of these colleges to identify those rural students from the office records. Once the Rural Students were identified from the lists of students provided by the colleges the population was compiled. The total number of Rural Students is 1138 of which 668 are male and 470 are female.

(c) **Sample:** The study was conducted among 32 rural science students which were selected by the used of the simple random sampling technique. Of the 32 Rural Students, 16 are male and 16 are female and also out of the 32 Rural Students, 17 students are in the 1st semester and 15 students are in 3rd semester.

(d) **Instrument**: The instrument used to gather the data for the pilot study was a closed-ended questionnaire which was constructed by the investigator.

Results of the Study

The data collected from the Rural Students by the use of a close-ended questionnaire was analyzed by the used of percentage and frequency. The results of this study are presented below:

Research Question 1: What are the problems faced by rural students in science education?

Objective 1: To study the problems faced by rural students in science education.

In order to study the problems faced by the rural students the data collected was analyzed using frequency and percentages. The results of objective 1 are presented by grouping the different problems faced by Rural Students in science education under the following components:

- Psychological Aspects
- Socio-Cultural Background
- Economic Status
- Quality of Available Physical Infrastructure
- Quality of Teachers

A. Psychological Aspects

Regarding the problems related to the psychological aspect, the study found that Rural Students faced a lot of stress and pressure in their pursuit of science education in higher education. One of the psychological aspects that affect the rural students in higher education was tension. The study revealed that 50% (16) of the students felt that pursuing higher education developed tension in them. The main source of pressure which causes tension among the Rural Students are their parents as 61% (21) of the students pointed out that they have been pressurised by their parents to get good grades. Another source that developed tension among the Rural

Students was communication as 78.10% (25) of the students get frustrated very when they cannot understand what was taught by the teachers. Also because of their busy schedule 78.10% (25) of the students commented that they often panic that they mightn't get the work done in time to meet deadlines as 68.75% (22) of the students find it stressful in handling the academic workload in college. The study also found that 62.50% (20) of the students felt terrified before going into the exams as 78.10% (25) find it stressful to study for examinations and 50% (16) have trouble concentrating in class. Moreover, 71.88% (23) of the Rural Students commented that the fear of failure in examination cause sleeplessness in them.

Another Psychological aspect that affects the Rural Students was their Self-concept. The study found that 50% (16) of the students felt that they were not as good as other students in the class; secondly 59.38% (19) felt that they cannot perform like anyone else in the class and thirdly 25% (8) of the Rural Students think they are academically inferior and cannot compete with urban students. However, it was noted that even thought Rural Students have an inferiority complex yet their educational aspiration was high. It was found that 90.63% (29) of the students believe that college education is important to get a job, 98.88% (31) believe that a college education is important to get ahead in life and 93.75% (30) believe that a college education is important to get a good standing in the society. In fact, 90.63% (29) of the students wanted to continue their education after graduation.

Low conceptual understanding was another problem related to the psychological aspect of the rural students in their pursuit of higher education. From the study conducted it was also found that Rural Students have a low conceptual understanding. It was revealed that 53.13% (17) of the Rural Students got easily distracted in the classroom. Also, 81.25% (26) of the students found it difficult to concentrate for a long period of time while studying. This study also revealed that 87.50% (28) of the students often have to read things several times before understanding them and 81.25% (26) find difficulty in remembering what they have learned.

B. Socio-Cultural Background

The socio-cultural background of the Students was another major problem faced by the Rural Students. One of the problems relating to the socio-cultural background of the rural students in pursuing science education at the higher level was the family background and support. The study conducted revealed that 31.03% (45) of the Rural Students were first generation learners i.e. they were first from their family to receive a college education and for some of them they were the first in the family to get an education. Hence, rural students do faced a problem due to the lack of support from their family regarding educational issues. The study conducted found that28.12% (9) of the Rural Students did not get any guidance from their family members regarding higher education and 65.62% (21) of the students revealed that their family members were not involve in making a decision about their course of study. This many times discourages the Rural Students as they don't have a role model at home. Rural Students also faced problems in discussing their college work at home as the family members do not understand and cannot help them as it was found that 59.38% (19) of the students never discuss their college work with their family members and 56.25% (18) never discuss the problems they faced in college with their family members. In fact, 71.88%(23) of the Rural Students expressed their desire for the family members to be more involved in their education.

Furthermore, involving the problems faced by the rural students in society and culture was their locale i.e. the place they belong. It was found that 9.38% (3) of the Rural Students commented that there are no college students in their locality which imply that no one from their locality has received a college education. This study also revealed that 18.15% (6) of the students felt that the elders in their locality do not give much priority to higher education as they are more concerned with the marriage and building of a family. Rural Students usually lack a mentor in their locality and this study confirmed this as it was found that 78.12% (25) of the students commented that they don't have a mentor in their locality to guide them in higher education. In fact, 53.12% (17) of the Rural Students pointed out that they don't have a college-educated role model in their locality. Indeed, 15.63% (5) of the Rural Students commented that they have been discouraged by people from their locality to pursue higher education.

Relating to the socio-cultural background another problem faced by Rural Students is lacked of peer support. In this study, it was found that 9.37% (3) of the Rural Students does not have friends to help them with their academic work as many of their friends are either in the other streams or have dropped out. In fact, 18.75% (6) of the Rural Students commented that their friends have discouraged them from pursuing higher education as they felt that doing well in college is not at all important.

Hence the lack of support from family, friends, and elders of the society add to the problems of the Rural Students in their pursuit of higher education.

C. Economic Status

Rural Students were often discouraged to pursue higher education is due to their economic status. Most of the families in rural areas are engaged in agriculture and most families are large in numbers. The fact that parents are uneducated and poor makes it more difficult for the Rural Students to opt for science education. From the study conducted it was found that 75% (24) of the Rural Students felt that the cost of higher education is a major concern for them in pursuing higher education. Rural Students also felt that their pursuance of higher education add to the burden of their family whose economic condition is not very high 75% (24) of the students felt that their quest for higher education adds to the burden of their family. This may be due to the fact that in Meghalaya the cost of science education is more than the cost of commerce and arts education. This study also revealed that 75% (24) of the Rural Students felt that the admission fee is a deciding factor for their admission into a college and they would choose a college that is cheaper so that they won't add to the economic burden of their families that's why we find a large number of Rural Students in those colleges where the fees of education is lesser than in those colleges where the fees is high. Moreover, because of the high cost of higher education, 15.6.3% (5) of the Rural Students revealed that they have taken a loan and 18.75% (6) have to work to support themselves. The study conducted also showed that 68.75% (22) of the Rural Students were not able to buy all the materials required for their course of study and that 78.13% (25) feel the cost of books is too expensive and books are important for students especially for science students.

Another issue related to economic problems faced by the students was the living cost. As there is a lack of colleges offering science education in the rural areas students who wish to take up science at the higher level have to migrate to the state capital where the colleges are mainly situated. The study revealed that of the 21 Rural Students who were staying in a rented house, 85.71% (18) find it very difficult to find a suitable low cost rented house and 52.38% (11) commented that they have to share accommodation with others because of the high cost of the rented house. In fact, the condition of the rented house according to 23.81% (5) of the students was not worth the rent paid for it. Similarly, of the 5 students who are staying in a hostel, 60% (3) revealed that the hostel fee and mess fee to be very expensive. Moreover, 37.50% (12) of the students indicated that the transport fees to be very expensive to travel to college.

D. Quality of the Available Physical Infrastructure

Regarding the quality of available infrastructure, only a few of the Rural Students have a problem. From the study conducted it was found that only 18.75% (6) of the students were not satisfied with the facilities of the classrooms in their college. The study also revealed that 12.50% (4) of the students felt that the condition of their classroom was not satisfactory and because of the unsatisfactory condition of the classroom 31.25% (10) of the students expressed that they cannot concentrate in the classroom. The main reason that Rural Students find difficulty in concentrating in the class was because of the unwanted noise as revealed by 43.75% (14) of the students.

Regarding the library, 6.25% (2) of the students commented that they never visit library and 40.62% (13) of the students revealed that they don't know how to search for books in the library. This study also revealed that 31.25% (10) of the Rural Students cannot get up-to-date books from the library. In fact, 34.38% (11) revealed that they cannot issue a sufficient number of books from the library.

Regarding the computer laboratory, 100% (32) of the students commented that their colleges have a computer laboratory. However, 15.62% (5) of the students indicated that they were not allowed to use the computers in the laboratory and 34.38% (11) of the students expressed that were not satisfied with the conditions of the computer laboratory. Moreover, 34.38% (11) of the rural students says that there was no one to help them in the computer laboratory.

With regard to the science laboratory, all the students commented that their colleges have a science laboratory. However, 25% (8) of the students commented that they were not satisfied with the science laboratory.

E. Quality of Teachers

Teachers are regarded as pillars of the educational system and the success of the systems depended so much on their quality. In the study the quality of the teachers was found to be one of the problems faced by the rural student in their pursuit for science education at the higher level. Regarding the quality of teachers, the study found that 9.38% (3) of the Rural Students felt that teachers do not have a mastery over the subject he/she is teaching. It was further revealed that 12.50% (4) of the students felt that the teacher does not help them to developed more interest in the subject he/she is teaching. Moreover, 6.25% (2) of the students felt the teachers were not flexible in their way of teaching so as to help all the students in the classroom. Further, 12.50% (4) of the students felt that the teachers do not provide a suitable example of concepts and skills.

The study also revealed that 15.62% (5) of the students felt that teachers do not engage the whole class while teaching in the classroom. It was also found that 28.12% (9) of the students commented that the teachers do not stimulate student thinking by asking a challenging question. Lastly, 53.13% (17) of the students reveal that the teacher does not make use of ICT to make the class interesting.

This study also found that 12.50% (4) of the Rural Students felt that the teachers were not friendly with the students and 3.12% (1) commended that teachers spoke negatively of students in the class. This study also found that 21.88% (7) of the Rural Students commented that the teachers were unapproachable by the students, 21.88% (7) of the Rural Students felt neglected by the teachers and 15.62% (5) were not comfortable in asking their teachers' help.

Objective 2: To study the challenges faced by rural students in science education.

Research Question 2: What are the challenges faced by rural students in science education?

The results of objective 2 are presents by grouping the different challenges faced by Rural Students in Science education into the following components:

- Transition
- Migration
- Adjusting to a Different Place and Different Teachers
- Language and Communication Barriers

A. Transition

The transition from school to college is a change that every student has to make in their quest for higher education. This study found that the transition from school to college also causes a challenge among Rural Students who pursue science education. The study revealed that 78.12% (25) of the students found the change from school to college very difficult. The main reasons for this was because Rural Students found college to be more academically challenging than high school as revealed by 81.25% (26) of the rural science students. There is a lacked of guidance to help rural students in their transition. In fact, the study showed that the rural science Students felt academically ill-prepared for college due to the poor quality of their higher secondary schools as revealed by 50% (16) of the students. Moreover the Rural science Students also needed more information before making a decision on which subject they should take up in college as commented by 87.50% (28) of the students. Thus, 56.36% (62) of the Rural Students find difficulty in adjusting to the academic demand of college and to efficiently manage their time in college as revealed by 56.25% (18) of the students. Another difficulty faced by the Rural Students in the transition period is the difference in the academic experience they had prior to joining college as revealed by 81.25% (26) of the students which affect the smooth transition into the colleges. Moreover, the changes from school to college also affect the academic performance of the students as revealed by 71.88% (23) of the students.

Apart from the academic transition, Rural Students also faced difficulty in making the social transition into college. The study found that 81.25% (26) of the students missed their old friends from schools when entering college as 40.62% (13) of the Rural Students feel isolated in college and 25% (8) do not feel a sense of belongingness. The study also found that 59.38% (19) of the students were afraid that they would not know anybody when they first join the college. Getting connected in a social group during the first year of college is also a challenge for many rural science Students as revealed by 40.62% (13) of the students. The study also showed that 37.50% (12) of the students felt disconnected with their friends and 71.88% (23) do not mix with classmates of the opposite sex in college. The study also found that 21.88% (7) believe that they were treated differently because of their rural background and34.38% (11) of the students felt discouraged in college and 43.75% (14) felt scared to seek out teacher's support in college.

B. Migration

Due to the lack of higher education institutions which offers course in science education in rural areas of Meghalaya, Rural Students who want to pursue science often have to migrate to another place in order to continue their education where they faced a lot of challenges. In this study out of

32 Rural Students who are from the science streams, 29 students have migrated to Shillong from their village in order to pursue their higher education. This study revealed that 68.97% (20) of the students find it very difficult to stay away from home in order to pursue their higher education. There were a number of reasons that makes Rural Students difficult to stay away from home; the first one is that living away from home Rural Students felt homesick as revealed by 65.52% (19) of the students as they missed their large family. Another reason was that since many of the parents of Rural Students are engaged in agriculture, the students felt bad that by moving away from home they cannot help their parents as they used to do as revealed by 79.31% (23) of the students. Therefore, 79.31% (23) of the Rural Students would prefer to stay close to their family in their own locality. The Rural Students who stayed away from home also revealed that being independent is also a challenge for them as55.17% (16) of the students finds difficulty in taking responsibility for their own self. Being independent is a challenge for students as 44.83% (13) of the students felt that by being away from home they lack the support that their parents provide. From this study, it was also found that by being away from home 55.17% (16) of the students felt a sense of disconnection with their family. It was also found that living away from home may also affect the educational performance of the students as revealed by 31.58% (36) of the students who felt that attachment to their family make it difficult for them to concentrate on their study.

C. Adjusting to a Different Place and Different Teachers

One of the major challenged faced by the rural science student was adjustment to the new place and teachers. The 29 Rural Students who migrate to Shillong for their higher studies also have difficulty in adjusting to this new place. Of the 29 Rural Students, 34.48% (10) of them find difficulty to adjust themselves in Shillong. The main reason for this as revealed by 37.93% (11) of the students was because they do not feel a sense of belongingness to the place. In fact, 31.03% (9) of the students felt like they are in the wrong place. The Rural science Students also have difficulty in adjusting because the people were not very sociable with them as revealed by 20.69% (6) of the students. Lastly, it was also revealed that 17.24% (5) of the students found it difficult to adapt to the weather condition of this place.

The Rural students also found it challenging to adjust to new teachers. The study revealed that 34.48% (10) of the rural science students found it difficult to adjust to their teacher's lecture in the classroom. Rural students also faced difficulty to adjust with the speed the new teacher teaches in the classroom as reveal by 48.28% (14) of the students. The way the teacher speaks or lecture also creates a challenge for the Rural Students as found by this study where 31.03% (17) of the students implied that it was difficult to adjust to the way their teachers talk. This study also found that 41.38% (12) of the students faced difficulty in adjusting to the academic demand of their teachers.

D. Language and Communication Barriers

Apart from the above mention challenges, Rural Students also face challenges regarding the use of English language as a medium of communication as most of the Rural Students have done their primary schooling in a Khasi or Garo medium schools and therefore does not have a proper background in English.The study revealed that 31.25% (10) of the Rural Students found it difficult to speak in English; this may be due to the fact that most Rural Students does not have enough practice to speak in the English language. Rural Students also lack vocabulary in English as 59.38% (19) of the Rural Students commented that they struggle to express themselves while writing in English and 50% (16) of the Rural Students found it difficult in understanding the meaning of the words used when someone speaks to them in English. The use of their mother tongue in their daily life and even in their school may also create a challenge for the Rural Students in speaking in English to others as 40.63% (13) of the Rural Students commented that they were not comfortable in speaking in English to their teachers inside the classroom. The study also revealed that 53.13% (17) of the Rural Students finds difficulty in communicating in English because of the used of their mother tongue.

Rural Students also faced a challenged in communicating with other due to many reasons. The study revealed that 71.88% (23) of the Rural Students indicated that they were afraid to give a presentation in class; this may be because they were not familiar with giving a presentation. The study also revealed that 28.13% (9) of the Rural Students do not participate in group discussions inside the classroom and as revealed by28.13% (9) of the students they have the fear of being incorrect, 56.25 (18) revealed that they felt too shy and 6.25% (2) do not participate because no opportunity was provided to them to participate in classroom discussion. Lastly, 81.25% (26) of the Rural Students have difficulty in communicating with faculty in the college, 18.75% (6) with the administrative staffs, 17.93% (26) with library in- charge and 4.83% (7) with the lab technician.

Suggestions for Improvement

Based on this study the following suggestion can be made so as to help Rural Students in their pursuit of science education:

1. Every Block in the state should have at least one higher education institutions which will offer courses in the Arts, Science and Commerce streams. This will help to decrease the migration of Rural Students to the state capital Shillong for higher education and will also help to minimize the cost of education for the Rural Students.
2. As far as possible the state government should try to improve the infrastructure in the rural areas and to encourage private college and universities offering science education to be established there.
3. Efforts should be made to forge links between science and other subjects, especially English and mathematics (Kaptan &Timurlenk, 2012).
4. Every college should have guidance and counseling cell as this study found that Rural Students in science education are facing a lot of psychological problems.
5. Every college who admit Rural Students either in the arts, commerce and science streams should organise an orientation programme before the starts of the semesters so that it will help the Rural Students to make a proper adjustment in their transition period.
6. Scholarships to the students from the rural areas should be provided and should be given at the beginning of the semesters since a majority of the Rural Students comes from a low socio-economic status family.
7. Short-term communication course should be organised by the college for those Rural Students who lack communication skills.

Conclusion

Science education is essential to realize the country's human resources potential to its fullest (Jahan & Selvarani, 2015). However, the findings of this study showed that Rural Students in Meghalaya faced a lot of problems and challenges in their pursuit of science education. In spite of the different difficulties that Rural Students faced it is heart-warming to see that majority of the Rural Students in this study wanted to continue their education after college and most of them said that they value education. Therefore, all effort should be made by all stakeholders including the government, educational institutions, teachers and parents to provide Rural Students with all the necessary guidance and assistance in their pursuit of science education, so that the rural youth can contribute not only to the development and prosperity of the rural areas but also to the State and Country as a whole.

The Government of Meghalaya has taken some step to make higher education in the various streams accessible to the people of rural areas and in December 2017 the Chief Minister of Meghalaya Shri Mukul Sangma announces that state government will invest Rs.50 crore for setting up of nine community colleges to make higher education accessible to the students of the state especially those from the rural areas. These community colleges are expected to decrease the migration of Rural Students to the state capital Shillong for higher education and also to ensure that students from rural areas have a dedicated college at their own backyards.

References

Akhtar, S. (2013). *Role of higher education in dealing with the socio-economic problems of Northeast India*. Retrieved from https://www.academia.edu/11474173/Role_of_Higher_Education_in_dealing_with_the_Socio-economic_Problems_of_Northeast_ India on 11-07-2017

Dash, T., & Mawthoh. I. (2010). Problems and prospects of higher education in rural areas of Meghalaya. *Educational Quest, International Journal of Education and Applied Social Sciences, 1* (1), 119-124.

Dwivedi, R. S., & Chakravarthy, R. V. (2015). Problems encountered by rural students in writing English- Role of English teacher- Some solutions. *International Journal on Studies in English Language and Literature, 3* (7), 27-38.

Kaptan, K., & Timurlenk, O. (2012). Challenges for science education. *Procedia-Social and Behavioral Sciences*, *51(2012)*, 763-771. doi: 10.1016/j.sbspro. 2012.08.237

Pheko, M. M., Monteiro, N., Tlhabano, K. N., & Mphele, S. B. (2014). Rural-to-urban migrations: Acculturation experiences among university students in Botswana. *International Journal of Adolescence and Youth, 19* (3), 306-317, DOI: 10.1080/02673843.2014.928782

Thyrniang, A. (2013, July 1st). Wanted more science and commerce institutes in rural Meghalaya. *The Shillong Times*. Retrieved from http://www.theshillongtimes.com/2013/07/01/wanted-more-science-and-commerce-institutes-in-rural-meghalaya/

Thyrniang, A. (2016, April 7th). MBOSE policy: Why go for soft option? The Shillong Times. Retrieved from http://www.theshillongtimes.com/2016/04/07/mbose-policy-why-go-for-soft-option/

UN Administrator (2013). *Challenges Facing Young Migrants*. Retrieved from https://www.un.org/esa/socdev/unyin/wyr/2013/report.pdf

Chapter - VI

Attitude towards Science and Achievement in Science: A Study among Higher Secondary School Students of Meghalaya

— *Lalmuanzuali & H.Malsawmi*

Introduction

There has been an increased proliferation of knowledge in the scientific and technological fields which necessitates the existence of a creative scientific community capable of developing advancements in science and technology. The revision and restructuring of science education from the school level can help in imparting better scientific skills and towards instilling a positive attitude towards science which can help in building a scientific community capable of keeping up with the on-going changes in science and technology.

The attitude of students towards science is an indispensable and significant topic in the field of scientific research and has acquired considerable interest among researchers. Attitude towards science may be referred to as a general and continuing positive or negative feeling about science. Yara (2009) has described the attitude towards science as an interest or feeling towards studying science. It is the students' disposition towards liking or disliking science. Osborne et al. (2003) have provided a list of components of attitude towards science. These components are "perception of the science teacher, anxiety towards science, the value of science, self-esteem at science, motivation towards science, enjoyment of science, attitudes of peers and friends towards science, the nature of classroom environment, achievement in science and fear of failure on course."

Attitudes are acquired instead of being inborn. The learning environment of the students, i.e. personal characteristics, school, classroom, teachers and family background have a substantial impact in shaping their attitude towards science. If students are guaranteed about acquiring successful experiences and positive feelings at the initial stage of their science education, they will be inspired and will likely have positive and fulfilling scientific experiences in the future. Thus, they will acquire a positive attitude towards science, and this will influence them to understand that learning of science is a lifelong pursuit. However, if students have negative experiences regarding their science education, they are more likely to develop a negative attitude towards science which they may carry on to the future years. (Simpson & Oliver, 1990)

Research findings consistently reveal attitudes as an essential component of science education that influences students' achievement (Joyce & Farenga, 2000; Osborne et al., 2003; Linn, 1992). Various studies have reported a high positive correlation between attitude towards science and science achievement (Wilson, 1983; Oliver & Simpson, 1988; Rana, 2002). High achievement scores were found among students with a positive attitude towards science (Hough & Piper, 1982; Wilson, 1983)

Science achievement has become a growing topic of concern in the field of education. Successful student achievement depends on various factors, such as the quality of schools and teachers, as well as attitude and aptitude amongst others. The ultimate objective of every teacher is to motivate the students to improve their ability level so that their success will be ensured.

In Meghalaya, the first attempt to introduce science education was through the recommendation of the first education commission appointed by the government in April 1972, which was then reconstituted in June 1975. Since then, science education has progressed at a steady pace within the state.

Attitude towards science as well as achievement in science is believed to be extremely important at the higher secondary stage because it is inclined to serve as a deciding factor for the selection of students' professional carriers. According to the Meghalaya Board of Secondary Education (2017-18), there were 74 higher secondary schools under

MBOSE offering science as a stream of education. Out of these higher secondary schools, 31 were in East Khasi Hills, within Shillong, which is the capital city. The rest of the schools were in the districts of East Garo Hills, East Jaintia Hills, North Garo Hills, RiBhoi, South Garo Hills, South West Garo Hills, West Garo Hills, West Jaintia Hills, West Khasi Hills, and South West Khasi Hills.

Rationale of the Study

Research findings show that attitude towards science and science achievement is positively correlated. Research in this field has been greatly stressed because of the increasing recognition that the national development of any country is largely determined by a highly educated, well-trained and adaptable workforce who takes part in the process of scientific and technological advancement. The enrolment of students taking science at the higher secondary stage in Meghalaya is much lower as compared to those in the arts stream. The low enrolment rates in the science stream have become a matter of great apprehension for the teaching community. Therefore the investigators felt it necessary to study the science achievement as well as attitude towards science among the higher secondary school students in Meghalaya. The present research work further tries to find out the correlation between attitude towards science and science achievement among higher secondary school students in Meghalaya.

Objectives

1. To find out the attitude towards science among higher secondary science students of Meghalaya.
2. To find out the science achievement among higher secondary science students of Meghalaya.
3. To find out the difference in the attitude towards science among higher secondary science students of Meghalaya with reference to gender.
4. To find out the difference in the science achievement among higher secondary science students of Meghalaya with reference to gender.
5. To find out the relationship between attitude towards science and science achievement among higher secondary school science students of Meghalaya.
6. To make suggestions for the improvement of science education in Meghalaya.

Hypotheses

1. There is no significant difference in the attitude towards science among higher secondary school science students of Meghalaya with reference to gender.
2. There is no significant difference in the science achievement among higher secondary school science students of Meghalaya with reference to gender.
3. There is no significant relationship between attitude towards science and science achievement among higher secondary school science students of Meghalaya.

Methodology

The causal comparative status survey design was employed for the present study. This is keeping in view the main objective which is to find out the attitude towards science as well as science achievement among higher secondary science students of Meghalaya and to compare their attitude and achievement with reference to their gender.

Tools Used

The following tools were used for the present study:

1. Science attitude scale developed by the investigators.
2. Achievement Test in Science (ATS-GR) developed by S.C. Gakhar and Rajnish; National Psychological Corporation Agra.

Population

The population for the present study consists of all the higher secondary school students offering science stream in Meghalaya

Sample

The sample comprises of 300 higher secondary school students randomly selected from the higher secondary schools offering science stream from the state of Meghalaya. Out of the total sample, 150 are males and 150 are females.

Analysis of Data

The data collected using science attitude scale as well as achievement test in science were tabulated and analysed, keeping in mind the objectives and hypotheses of the study.

Attitude towards Science among Higher Secondary School Science Students

The scores of all higher secondary school science students on science attitude scale were scored and tabulated. Based on their responses, the students were classified into three groups as per the norms of the scale. The scores above the 75th percentile constitute positive attitude, those below the 25th percentile constitute negative attitude and those between the 25th and 75th percentile constitute moderate attitude. The following Table - 6.1 shows the position of higher secondary school science students of Meghalaya with respect to their attitude towards science.

Table 6.1: Science Attitude among Higher Secondary School Students of Meghalaya

Science Attitude	*Total (N=300)*	
	No. of Students	*Percentage*
Positive Attitude (80-100)	73	24.33 %
Neutral Attitude (68-79)	146	48.66 %
Negative Attitude (8-67)	81	27 %

Table - 6.1 reveals that out of 300 higher secondary school students of Meghalaya, 73 (24.33%) students have a positive attitude towards science, 146 (48.66%) have a neutral attitude towards science, and 81 (27%) have a negative attitude towards science. The above table further shows that the majority of the students have a neutral attitude towards science. There were more students with a positive attitude towards science than with a negative attitude.

Science Achievement among Higher Secondary School Science Students

The Achievement Test in Science (ATS-GR) developed by S.C. Gakhar and Rajnish was administered to the higher secondary school science students and the scores obtained were scored and tabulated. The scores above the 75th percentile constitute high achievement, those below the 25th percentile constitute low achievement, and those between the 25th and 75th percentile constitute average achievement. The following Table - 6.2 shows the position of higher secondary school science students in Meghalaya with respect to their science achievement.

Table 6.2: Science Achievement among Higher Secondary School Students of Meghalaya

Science Achievement	*Score Range*	*Total (N=300)*	
		No. of Students	*Percentage*
High Achievement	20 - 32	59	19.66%
Average Achievement	14 - 19	143	47.66%
Low Achievement	5 -13	98	32.66%

Table No – 6.2 shows that out of 300 higher secondary school students of Meghalaya, 59 (19.66 %) students have high science achievement, 143 (47.66 %) students have average science achievement, and 98 (32.66 %) students have low science achievement. Hence, the majority of the students have average achievement in science. The numbers of students with high achievement in science are slightly more in number than those with low achievement in science.

Gender Difference in Attitude towards Science among Higher Secondary School Science Students

To compare the attitude towards science between the male and female higher secondary school students the mean and standard deviation of both the males and females were calculated. The t-value was then established in order to ascertain the difference between the two groups. The following Table - 6.3 shows the comparison in the attitude towards science among higher secondary school science students of Meghalaya with reference to gender.

Table 6.3: Attitude towards Science among Higher Secondary School Students of Meghalaya with reference to Gender

Gender	*N*	*Mean*	*SD*	*MD*	*SEMD*	*t-value*	*Sig. level*
Male	150	70.57	11.355				
Female	150	73.71	9.974	3.140	1.234	2.545	0.05

As shown in the above Table - 6.3, the ‘t’ value for the significance of the difference between mean attitude scores of male and female higher secondary school students of Meghalaya towards science is 2.545. Since the calculated ‘t’ value was greater than the criterion ‘t’ value, there was a significant difference in the attitude of higher secondary school students of Meghalaya with reference to gender. Therefore, the hypothesis that there is no significant difference in the attitude towards science among higher secondary school students of Meghalaya with reference to gender was rejected as there was a significant difference at the 0.05 level. A comparison of their mean score shows that female students have a more positive attitude towards science than male students.

Gender Difference in Science Achievement of Higher Secondary School Science Students of Meghalaya

The mean and standard deviation of the achievement scores of male and female higher secondary school science students was also calculated. The significance of difference between the means was tested, by applying t-test. Table - 6.4 displays the comparison of the science achievement of higher secondary science students of Meghalaya with respect to gender.

Table 6.4: Science Achievement of Higher Secondary School Students of Meghalaya with reference to Gender

Gender	*N*	*Mean*	*SD*	*MD*	*SEMD*	*t-value*	*Sig. level*
Male	150	16.25	5.144	.487	.539	.902	NS
Female	150	15.76	3.869				

NS means not significant.

Looking at Table - 6.4 it was found that the 't' value for the significance of the difference between the mean scores of male and female students of Meghalaya towards Science Achievement is .902, whereas the required 't' value with df = 298, to declare the difference as significant is 1.97 at 0.05 level of confidence. Since the calculated 't' value was lower than the criterion 't' value, there exists no significant difference in the science achievement of higher secondary school students of Meghalaya with reference to gender. Therefore, the null hypothesis that there is no significant difference in the science achievement among higher secondary school students of Meghalaya with reference to gender was accepted.

Relationship between Attitude towards Science and Science Achievement among Higher Secondary School Students of Meghalaya

The Pearson Product Moment Correlation Method was used to determine the correlation between attitude towards science and science achievement among all higher secondary school students of Meghalaya. Table No. 6.5 presents the correlation between attitude towards science and science achievement among higher secondary science students of Meghalaya.

Table 6.5: Correlation between Attitude towards Science and Science Achievement among Higher Secondary School Students of Meghalaya.

Categories	*Attitude*	*Achievement*
Attitude	1	0.132*
Achievement	0.132*	1

* Significant at 0.05 level; N=300.

As revealed in Table - 6.5 the correlation between attitude towards science and science achievement among higher secondary school students of Meghalaya was found to be positive and significant ($r = .132, p < 0.05$) at 0.05 level of confidence. Therefore, the null hypothesis that there is no significant relationship between attitude towards science and science achievement among higher secondary school students of Meghalaya was rejected. Therefore, there was a slight positive correlation between the two variables, which implies that the more positive the attitude of the students towards science, the higher their science achievement and vice versa.

Suggestions

1. Teachers should possess positive attitude towards science because their performances are deeply affected by their perception of science. Teachers should undergo pre-service and in-service trainings so as to increase their perception of science in a favourable way. This will further help cultivate a positive attitude towards science among their students.
2. Improvement of science achievement should remain a priority in the teaching community so as to train the youth to become well-informed and effective citizens equipped with critical and analytical thinking skills, contributing to the social and economic prosperity of our respective states, and consequently to our country.
3. In order to develop positive science attitude and draw more students towards science subject, the co-curricular activities of the schools should include activities like science exhibitions, science quiz, science projects, science debates, etc.
4. The schools should have well equipped science clubs at the higher secondary stage.
5. Scholarships and other incentives awarded to meritorious science students should be raised by the state Governments.

6. Schools should have well equipped laboratories, good libraries, high quality science teaching aids, etc. so as to increase larger participation of students in science related activities.
7. Parents should not undermine the scientific abilities of their daughters. Equal treatment should be given to both sons and daughters.

References

Ali, M. S., & Awan, A. S. (2013). Attitude towards science and its relationship with students achievement in science.*Interdisciplinary Journal of Contemporary Research in Business, 4*(10), 707719. Retrieved from https://journal-archieves28.webs.com/707- 718.pdf

Ahuja, A. (2017). Study of scientific attitude in relation to science achievement scores among secondary school students.*Educational Quest - An International Journal of Education and Applied Social Sciences, 8*(1), 9. doi:10.5958/2230-7311.2017.00002.2

Akpýnar, E., Yýldýz, E., Tatar, N., & Ergin, Ö. (2009). Students' attitudes toward science and technology: An investigation of gender, grade level, and academic achievement. *Procedia - Social and Behavioral Sciences, 1*(1), 2804-2808. doi:10.1016/j.sbspro.2009.01.498

Benny, A. (1990). A study of the relationship of critical thinking, science aptitude and socio-economic status to the science achievement of second year PUC students. *Fifth Survey of Educational Research 1988-1992*, II. New Delhi: NCERT.

Darchhingpuii. (1989). A study of science achievement, science attitude and problem-solving ability among secondary school students in Aizawl. *Fifth Survey of Educational Research 1988-1992*, II. New Delhi: NCERT.

Eysenck, H. J., Arnold, W., & Meili, R. (1975). *Encyclopedia of psychology*. London: Fontana/Collins in association with Search Press.

Hough, L. W., & Piper, M. K. (1982). The relationship between attitudes toward a science and science achievement. *Journal of Research in Science Teaching, 19*(1), 33-38. doi:10.1002/tea.3660190105

Jayasri, B. (1984). *Environmental influence, academic achievement and scientific aptitude as determinants of adolescents' attitude towards science stream.* (Unpublished doctoral thesis) University of Calcutta, Kolkata.

Joyce, B.A., & Farenga, S.J. (2000). Young girls in science: Academic ability, perceptions, and future participation in science. *Roper Review*, *22*(4), 261-262.

Linn, M.C. (1992). Science education reform: Building the research base. *Journal of Research in Science Teaching, 29,* 821-840.

Malsawmi, H. (2010). *Progress and Expansion of Education in Mizoram- An Analysis. Aizawl*, Mizoram: JP Offset Printers and Publishers.

Oliver, J.S., & Simpson, R.D. (1988). Influences of attitude toward science, achievement motivation, and science self-concept on achievement in science:

A longitudinal study. *Science Education, 72*(2), 143-155. doi:10.1002/sce.3730720204

Oliver, J.S., Simon, S., & Collins, S. (2003). Attitude towards science: A review of the literature and its implications. *International Journal of Science Education, 25*(9), 1049-1079.

Osborne, J., Simon, S., & Collins, S. (2003). Attitudes towards science: A review of the literature and its implications. International Journal of Science Education, *25*(9), 1049-1079. doi:10.1080/0950069032000032199

Rana, R.A. (2002). *Effect of parents, socioeconomic status, students, self-concept and gender on science related attitudes and achievement* (Unpublished doctoral thesis). Institute of Education and Research, University of the Punjab, Lahore.

Simpson, R. D., & Oliver, J. S. (1990). A summary of major influences on attitude toward and achievement in science among adolescent students. *Science Education, 74*(1), 1-18. doi:10.1002/sce.3730740102

Willson, V. L. (1983). A meta-analysis of the relationship between science achievement and science attitude: kindergarten through college. *Journal of Research in Science Teaching, 20*(9), 839-850. doi:10.1002/tea.3660200906

Yara, O.P. (2009). Students' attitude towards mathematics and academic achievement in some selected secondary schools in south western Nigeria. *European Journal of Scientific Research, 36*(3), 336-341.

Chapter - VII

How Emotions Influence Students' Achievement in Science? An Analysis in the Context of Mizoram

— Nitu Kaur & R. P. Vadhera

Emotions and their Connection with Science

The emotions are like mirror image of one's mind-set. They reflect the reactions of the individual towards a particular stimulus. A healthy emotional profile of learner is a very important pre-requisite for the good performance in academics. There is a certain amount of positive relationship between the involvement of emotions in teaching–learning situation and level of student's achievement in different subjects. It is very obvious that having healthy emotions is a prime cause for mental well being of learners. The National Institute for Health and Care Excellence (NICE), England has used the term 'mental wellbeing' in its work on children's mental health. Its definition of mental wellbeing is subdivided into three dimensions: emotional wellbeing, psychological wellbeing and social wellbeing. Children's 'mental wellbeing' encompasses three domains as defined by NICE (Adi et al. 2007), (i) Emotional wellbeing (including happiness and confidence, and the opposite of depression/anxiety); (ii) Psychological wellbeing (including resilience, mastery, confidence, autonomy, attentiveness/involvement and the capacity to manage conflict and to problem solve); and (iii) Social wellbeing (good relationships with others, and the opposite of conduct disorder, delinquency, interpersonal violence and bullying). It has been evidenced through research that physical, cultural and emotional health and the school environment in which teaching and learning are expected to occur dramatically impact a student's ability to succeed.

Berger et al. (2010) tried to investigate the effect of emotional wellbeing on academic achievement which was an overlooked perspective pertaining to the fact that traditionally schools are solely focusing on cognitive development and academic training of students for showing educational outcomes. They adopted a multilevel perspective to test this association among Chilean elementary students, considering features at individual (socio-emotional well- being, self esteem, and social integration) and social levels (classroom social climate and social network characteristics). Results of the study showed significant correlations between socio-emotional wellbeing, self esteem, social integration and a positive perception of the school social climate, and academic achievement. In particular teachers' ratings of their students' self esteem is strongly associated with academic achievement. According to Barry et al. (2015) within the context of schools, Social and Emotional Learning (SEL) involves the integration of two interrelated strands to promote successful school performance and youth development which are (i) skills development and (ii) supportive environments. Pekrun et al. (2002) in an extensive qualitative study found that students experience a rich diversity of academic emotion. Their research review confirmed that academic emotions have largely been neglected with an exception of test anxiety. They developed an Academic Emotions Questionnaire (AEQ) and it was tested in 7 cross-sectional, 3 longitudinal, and 1 diary study using samples of university and school students. The findings of the study confirmed that academic emotions are significantly related to students' academic achievement, motivation, learning strategies, cognitive resources and self-regulation. Hence the importance emotions cannot be undermined in educating children.

Science teaching-learning process equally demands the emotional wellbeing of learners so that they can achieve the maximum out of the subject. Affective domain of learner is traditionally placed at the backseat in the science classroom owing to popular assumptions that emotions threaten the neutrality of truth, which the discipline of science aims to search and validate. When it comes to teaching-learning process in science classroom, the situation is far more displeasing.

Reiss (2005) said that emotions are vital factors in deciding the fate of students in science but sadly a very little attention has been given to emotions in sciences in the recent past. Science has been strictly associated with the learners' cognitive abilities and emotions find a very little mention in science classrooms. In maximum instances they are ignored owing to the ignorance of teachers and others practicing science. They argue that emotions interfere with the neutrality of knowledge and may shade knower's thought which can be a limit in search of truth. In recent past many counter arguments have surfaced due to a long ignorance of one's emotions especially in the field of science. Scientists are also passionate beings who strive to live their dream of unfolding the mysteries of the nature and in doing so their emotions guide them to the foremost. Alsop (2001) claimed that contemporary school science is being portrayed as rational and non-emotional in recent times consistently overlooking the aspect of affect in studying and doing science. Alsop & Watts (2003) confirmed through their study that science education is not limited to cognition rather it becomes more meaningful when it targets the affect of the learners. Further, Abrahams (2009) through his study suggested that there are affective components in doing science along with cognitive.

Watts & Alsop (1997) in their series of empirical studies explored nature of learners' understanding, their identification with science and scientific issues and their reactions to 'radiation and radioactivity' topics within science. Their study revealed that science concepts should be taught in such a way that they seem agreeable to mind or palatable; where they found evidence after interviewing students that unpalatable concepts undergo 'conceptual avoidance'. They argued that the conceptual change view of learning is as much dependent on the affective domain as much as on the cognitive. Brígido et al. (2013) in their descriptive and comparative study on the emotions about teaching and learning science in three Spanish universities found that the prospective teachers felt positive emotions towards learning subjects of Geology/ Biology and negative towards learning subjects of Physics/ Chemistry when they recalled their secondary school days but they expected in their future teaching positive emotions will increase and negative emotions will decrease than they used to feel at secondary school levels. They suggested that in science education affective aspect should be given importance at par with cognitive.

It can be concluded after reviewing the above studies that the role of emotions has been mostly in the compromised state when it comes to teaching-learning situations in science. In social sciences and languages, the role of affect has been always utilized and it is also very much in the character of these disciplines that affect finds an inbuilt composition in their delivery. But it is very sad that science as a discipline sometime becomes very hostile for students and they treat it as a dry discipline which is not the case. There is a serious need to change this notion and take the advantage of one's affect in making science teaching-learning experience more meaningful for both students and teachers.

Emotional Stability: A Competent Factor Influencing One's Personality

The term 'emotional well being' is being frequently spelled in recent literature which overlaps with the psychological construct of emotional stability. Research has confirmed that one of the variables determining the good performance of students in science is their emotional wellbeing which also highlights the importance of emotional stability of the learners. The emotions associated with vivid life experiences may facilitate or hinder the teaching-learning process. Hence emotional stability is a desirable quality for fruitful learning outcomes. The emotional wellbeing of students needs to be studied in depth as it relate to their emotional stability. The emotional stability of students may have a positive impact on their achievement in science. There seems to be a positive correlation between positive emotions and academic achievement. Similarly it can be linked with students' achievement in science.

The root of emotional stability as a psychological construct is derived from type and trait theories of personality. Particularly Cattell's trait theory and Eysenck's type theory need to be mentioned for their contributions in personality theories. Both these theories recognize emotional stability as one of the trait or type of personality respectively in their explanation. Cattell et al. (1970) identified 16 Personality Factors (16PF) and developed a questionnaire on personality assessment wherein subject responses are scored on variability of responses on personality traits kept on a continuum from low to high score description. One of the factor named as C describes being emotionally stable and facing reality as a high score description in comparison to being affected by feelings and getting easily upset as a low score description. Similarly Eysenck chose certain personality dimensions on which individuals are assumed to vary, which he defined as personality type. His personality system comprises of four dimensions viz. Intelligence as the only cognitive dimension, extraversion- introversion, neuroticism-stability and psychoticism-stability. The causal factors in Eysenck's theory, are deeply rooted in biology, are highly complex and heavily relies on initial work of Pavlov, 1927 and Hull, 1943 (Peck & Whitlow, 1975).

The neuroticism dimension is similar to the notion of emotional instability (Peck & Whitlow, 1975). It means individuals who fall at the extreme end of neuroticism dimension tend to be more susceptible to worries, anxieties and under extreme stressful conditions are prone to develop neurotic disorders whereas the opposite extreme end defines a highly emotional stable state. The background of these two personality theories clearly defines emotional stability as highly desired mental state which contributes towards the wellbeing of the individual in holistic way. Emotional stability is one of the five personality traits of the Big Five personality theory which identifies five factors of personality as Extraversion, Agreeableness, Conscientiousness, Neuroticism, and Openness to Experience based on Five Factor Model (FFM) as designated by Goldberg in 1981 (McCrae & John, 1991). Emotional stability is measured through the factor Neuroticism. Emotional stability refers to a person's ability to remain stable and balanced. At the other end of the scale, a person who is high in neuroticism has a tendency to easily experience negative emotions.

According to Chaturvedi & Chander (2010) Emotional instability or immaturity points to an individual's failure to develop the degree of independence or self-reliance that is seen in a normal adult, with consequent use of immature adjustive patterns and inability to maintain equilibrium under stresses, unlike most individuals who do not have these negative traits.

This means that values like tolerance, patience, dedication and commitment, flexibility and not over expecting from every situation are some of the desirable virtues of an emotionally sound and stable personality. These virtues also facilitate the spirit to scientific enquiry. They foster the scientific temper and zeal to know more. Similarly, an emotionally stable child has the capacity to make effective adjustment with himself, members of his family, and his peers in school, society and culture.

Studies also report that emotional stability is a highly varying trait and is associated with gender as well. According to Aleem (2005) the male students are more emotionally stable than the females due to many intervening factors influencing the emotions of females. It poses an obvious question in mind, are emotions gendered? This leads to further more curious queries with regard to gender studies. Very few studies could be documented covering the aspect of emotional stability or maturity in India and no study was conducted for understanding the relationship between learners' emotional stability and science achievement. As far as western studies are concerned a lot of studies in context of emotions (affect) and their role in science education has been a prime focus area of research since 1980s. Therefore review of relevant literature suggests that there is a need to study the relationship between one's emotions and their science education and further to their achievement in science, especially in indigenous setting. The present investigation in thus guided by some of the following underlying questions which are:

1. Do emotions really matter in the field of science, and if yes in what way it might be associated with understanding, doing, philosophizing and practicing science?
2. Do emotionally sound and stable students are able to achieve better scores in science?
3. How does gender influence the emotional state of the learners and their achievement in science?

Operational Definitions Used for the Present Study

Emotional Stability: In the present study the term Emotional Stability refers to, "individuals' steadiness of mood and ability to remain calm when faced with pressure or stress" *Achievement in Science*: Here the term achievement refers to the extent of attainment of science concepts by the students at the secondary level of education. The MBSE (Mizoram Board of School Education) results of class X are taken as the criterion of the students' achievement in science.

Population & Sample

For the present study all the MBSE (Mizoram Board of School Education) affiliated class X secondary school students of Aizawl district formed the target population. The chosen sample comprised of 1134 secondary school students (532 boys and 602 girls) of class X from 34 MBSE affiliated schools in Aizawl district of Mizoram, India. Random cluster sampling technique was used to pool out the sample. High schools were chosen randomly as a sample unit while data collection. Each sampling unit became a student cluster of sample from where data was collected from the available secondary school students of class X.

Sources of Data

The present study has made use of both primary and secondary data. The primary data comprises of sample of class X students and secondary data comprised of data from annual publication on secondary schools, MBSE. The school visits were finalized using data from secondary sources.

Science Achievement Scores

The class X board results 2016-17 of the sampled population was procured through MBSE office to obtain their scores in science subject which was pre-decided as the parameter of their science achievement. This was also a secondary data.

Instrument Used

The data for the present study was collected using a self-constructed Emotional Stability Scale (ESS) for measuring the emotional stability of secondary school students. Although some standardized questionnaires and scales were available, it was decided by the investigator to construct a scale on own which could be easily answered by the secondary school students with the possibility of using simplified statements for items. The choice of construction of the scale is justified because the available scales were either very lengthy to be administered and some of the scales were not compatible to the present sample. The emotional stability scale tried to measure the student's feeling and emotional response upon reading various situational statements through the preferential choice of any of the three provided options which were 'Often', 'Sometimes' or 'Rarely'. Since there were both positive and negative statements in the scale the corresponding weighted score for positive statements will be 3, 2, 1 respectively for 'often', 'sometimes' or 'rarely' and for negative statements will be 1, 2, 3 respectively for 'often', 'sometimes' or 'rarely'. After the construction of first draft of scale it was tried out on small sample and item analysis was performed. Item discrimination index for each item was calculated by using t-test (Guilford, 1979). Items found insignificant in their discrimination power at 0.05 level of significance were discarded and rest items were retained for the final draft of the scale. In the final draft there were 18 positive and 9 negative items. Therefore the maximum possible score on ESS is 81 (3x27) and minimum score is 27(1x27).

The final draft of the emotional stability scale was subjected to reliability testing. Reliability was obtained both by split-half and odd-even method which was found respectively as 0.561 and 0.701 respectively after applying Spearman-Brown formula both of which is an acceptable value for reliability for measuring affective trait like emotional stability. Also the test-retest method was also employed to have further assessment of reliability. The gap kept between the test and retest was kept approximately a month. The test-retest reliability was found to be 0.68. The Cronbach Alpha coefficient for internal consistency on test and retest were found 0.562 and 0.432 respectively. This was also moderately acceptable reliability.

In order to establish the content validity of the final draft scale opinion was sought from eight experts from the field of psychology. The items were found to be valid for the chosen purpose of the scale and easy to comprehend.

Objectives of the Study

Following are the objectives of the present study:

1. To compare the high and low achievers in science in relation to their emotional stability amongst the secondary school students.
2. To examine the gender variation in emotional stability amongst the secondary school students.
3. To examine the gender variation in science achievement amongst the secondary school student.
4. To find out the gender differences within high and low achievers in science in relation to their emotional stability amongst the secondary school students.

Research Hypotheses

The following are the research hypothesis based on the review of the relevant literature:

1. High achievers in science have higher level emotional stability whereas low achievers in science have a lower level of emotional stability.
2. There is a significant difference in emotional stability with respect to gender.
3. There is significant gender difference with respect to science achievement.
4. (a) There is significant difference in emotional stability of high achievers with respect to gender.

   (b) There is significant difference in emotional stability of low achievers with respect to gender.

Analysis and Interpretation of Data

In the light of objectives of the study the collected data was scored, tabulated and analyzed using differential analysis of independent t-test as the data obtained on the trait of emotional stability was found to be normally distributed with a mean, median and mode of 57.6, 57 & 56 respectively and value of skewness and kurtosis of 0.237(SES=0.073) & -0.030 (SEK=0.145) respectively. A general guideline for skewness is that if the number is greater than +1 or lower than –1, this is an indication of a substantially skewed distribution (Hair et al., 2017, p. 61). Applying this guideline the skewness value (.237) qualifies to be within the limits of normality. For kurtosis, the general guideline is that if the number is greater than +1, the distribution is too peaked. Likewise, a kurtosis of less than –1 indicates a distribution that is too at (Hair et al., 2017, p. 61). Applying this guideline the kurtosis value (-.030) qualifies to be within the limits of normality. Similarly students' science score were also found to be near-normally distributed with a mean, median and mode of 57.04, 56 & 47 respectively and value of skewness and kurtosis of .110 (SES=.073) & -.481 (SEK=.145) respectively which is acceptable for fulfilling the assumptions of normality (Hair et al., 2017).

Following are the objective wise analysis of data with appropriate interpretation. Mainly data was subjected to differential analysis to find out the answers of the research question.

A. Differential Analysis between High and Low Achievers in Science

Procedure Adopted for Classification of High and Low Achievers in Science:

For classification of selected sample students into high and low achievers the science achievement scores of all 1134 students was arranged in descending order and the top 27% were taken as high achievers and bottom 27% were be taken as low achievers. Thus the size of the sample of high and low achievers in science became 306 top achievers and 306 bottom achievers making a total of 612 students.

Objective 1: To compare the high and low achievers in science in relation to their emotional stability.

The research questions guided to propose null hypothesis in order to statistically test it. the null hypothesis is as follows:

Ho1:-There is no significant difference between low and high achievers in science with respect to emotional stability.

The emotional stability scores of the two groups were subjected to differential analysis. For the testing of hypothesis student 't' test (independent sample) was performed (Table 7.1).

Table 7.1: Significance of Difference between High and Low Achievers in Science in Relation to their Emotional Stability

Group	*Number*	*Mean*	*S.D.*	*S.E.M.*	*T value*	*df*	*Significance of Difference*	*Decision on Null Hypothesis*
High Achievers	306	59.18	5.152	0.2945	7.945	610	S**	Rejected
Low Achievers	306	56.04	4.611	0.2636				

Source: Field data, **The test suggests that the difference between the two means is extremely significant at 0.01 level.

Interpretation: A reference to Table 7.1 reveals that there is statistically significant difference between the mean emotional stability scores of high achievers in science (M=59.18, SD=5.152) and the mean emotional stability scores of low achievers in science (M= 56.04, SD=4.611); obtained t value (7.945) was found extremely significant at 0.01 level with degree of freedom 610,'t' critical value (2.576) being < obtained 't' value. It means that emotional stability of secondary school students vary between low and high achievers. The emotional stability of high achievers is greater than that of low achievers. Hence the null hypothesis is rejected.

B. Differential Analysis between Boys and Girls

Objective 2: To examine the gender variation in emotional stability amongst the secondary school students.

The research question guided to propose the following null hypotheses:

Ho2:-There is no significant gender difference in secondary school students with respect to their emotional stability.

Table 7.2: Significance of Difference between Boys and Girls in Relation to their Emotional Stability

Group	*Number*	*Mean*	*S.D.*	*S.E.M.*	*t value*	*df*	*Significance of Difference*	*Decision on Null Hypothesis*
Boys	532	57.97	5.174	0.2243	2.27	1132	S*	Rejected
Girls	602	57.27	5.072	0.2067				

Source: Field data. *The test suggests that the difference between the two means is significant at 0.05 level.

Interpretation: A reference to Table 7.2 reveals that the obtained t value (2.27) was found significant at 0.05 level with degree of freedom 1132, 't' critical value(1.96) being < obtained 't' value. It means that emotional stability of secondary school students vary with respect to their gender with boys being more emotionally stable. Hence the null hypothesis is rejected.

Objective 3: To examine the gender variation in science amongst the secondary school student.

For the given objective the science achievement scores of students were compared with respect to their gender. Following null hypothesis was proposed:

Ho3:-There is no significant gender difference in the secondary school students with respect to science achievement.

Table 7.3: Significance of Difference between Boys and Girls in Relation to their Achievement in Science

Group	*Number*	*Mean*	*S.D.*	*S.E.M.*	*t value*	*df*	*Significance of Difference*	*Decision on Null Hypothesis*
Boys	532	58.748	14.324	0.6210	3.62	1132	S**	Rejected
Girls	602	55.522	15.511	0.6322				

Source: Field data, **The test suggests that the difference between the two means is extremely significant at 0.01level.

Interpretation: A reference to Table 7.3 reveals that the obtained t value (3.62) was found significant at 0.01 level with degree of freedom 1132, 't' critical value (2.576) being < obtained 't' value. It means that science achievement of secondary school students vary with respect to their gender. The science achievement of boys is better than girls. Hence the null hypothesis is rejected.

C. Gender Differences within High and Low Achievers in Science

Objective 4: *To find out the gender differences within high and low achievers in science in relation to their emotional stability.*

Gender comparison was also done within high (top 306) and low (bottom 306) achieving groups using t test for the testing of following null hypotheses. There were 156 boys and 150 girls in the high achieving group. Similarly there were 120 boys and 186 girls in the low achieving group. Following null hypotheses were proposed for the given objective:

Ho4a:-There is no significant difference in emotional stability of high achievers with respect to gender.

Ho4b:- There is no significant difference in emotional stability of low achievers with respect to gender.

Table 7.4: Significance of Difference between Boys and Girls within High and Low Achieving Groups of Science in Relation to their Emotional Stability (ES)

Group	*Number*	*Mean*	*S.D.*	*S.E.M.*	*t value*	*df*	*Significance of Difference*	*Decision on Null Hypothesis*
ES of High Achieving Boys	156	59.74	5.01	0.401	1.973	304	S*	*Ho4a* Rejected
ES of High Achieving Girls	150	58.59	5.25	0.429				
ES of Low Achieving Boys	120	55.48	4.26	0.389	1.689	304	NS	*Ho4b* Accepted
ES of Low Achieving Girls	186	56.39	4.80	0.352				

Source: Field data *The test suggests that the difference between the two means is significant at 0.05 level. NS suggests that that the difference between the two means is not significant at 0.05 level.

Interpretation: A reference to Table 7.4 reveals that after the comparison between means on emotional stability of boys and girls within the high achieving groups the obtained t value (1.973) was found significant at 0.05 level with degree of freedom 304, 't' critical value(1.960) being < obtained 't' value. It means that there is variation in emotional stability of students within the high achieving groups with respect to their gender. The mean score of boys on emotional stability is higher than that of girls. Hence the null hypothesis (Ho4a) is rejected.

A similar comparison within the low achieving groups was also performed. Again with reference to Table 7.4 the obtained t value (1.689) was found not significant at 0.05 level with degree of freedom 304, 't' critical value(1.960) being > obtained 't' value. It means that there is no variation in emotional stability of students within the low achieving groups with respect to their gender. Hence the null hypothesis (Ho4b) is accepted.

Discussion

Differential analysis in the present study in context of Mizoram revealed that emotional stability of secondary school students vary between low and high achievers in science. It was found that the emotional stability of high achievers is greater than that of low achievers. This finding is slightly in agreement with one Indian comparative study done by Lal (1968) where it was found that the superior pupils in terms of their academic achievement had a slightly better tendency towards adjustment in general however the difference was not significant. Further it reported that at 14+ and 15+ of age the superior pupils were better adjusted whereas at 16+ of age the average group was better adjusted which suggested that while emotional stability increased with age in the superior group, it deteriorated with age in the average group.

Further the present study revealed that the emotional stability of secondary school students vary with respect to their gender such that boys were more emotionally stable than the girls. On further analysis on the comparison of emotional stability within the high achieving group also confirmed that emotional stability varied with regard to gender, wherein high achieving boys were found to be more emotionally stable than their counter parts. However a similar comparison within low achieving group showed that emotional stability did not varied with regard to gender which may be because of less influence of emotional stability as an affective factor on the students' achievement in science within this group. Girls in the superior group were ruled by immediate need of gratification to sustain positive emotions, but boys in the same group were ruled to a lesser degree for the need of gratification and they also showed a less withdrawing type of behavior in comparison to their counterparts. In Indian context this study reconfirmed the findings of Aleem (2005) wherein it was found that the male undergraduate students are more emotionally stable than the females which may be due to the fact that females are more susceptible as result of feelings of insecurity, lack of ability to adjust.

As far as the gender differences with respect to students' achievement in science are concerned the present findings are again in favour of boys who performed significantly better than the girls. This further strengthens the linkage of good performance in science with a sound capability of being emotionally stable. This means a sound emotionally stable state may contribute positively towards high achievement in science and science education in general. All the investigations in the past further help to associate the linkage between one's emotion and science. Emotional stability is a positive trait of personality that guides a person towards a healthy interaction with all objects in the environment both inanimate and animate that help him/her to cope with unfavourable conditions. Present findings are very much is in conformity with the guiding research hypothesis that high achievers in science have higher level emotional stability whereas low achievers in science have a lower level of emotional stability. Also it confirmed the second and third research hypotheses that there is a significant difference in emotional stability and achievement in science of secondary school students with respect to their gender. Gender differences also prevailed within high achieving group with boys being better on the trait of emotional stability.

Conclusion

Emotional stability is an ability of person to face unfavourable situations of life with calmness and steadiness. It is one of the prominent factors determining a healthy persona. A student's achievement in science can be enhanced if the emotions of students are given space in classroom along with cognition as it helps to bring liveliness and attachment with the subject. Emotional stability as a trait can help students' achievement in science provided their emotions are healthy, positive and strong to positively contribute towards their performance in science. Unhealthy class environment, biased teacher behaviour and inert dry science curriculum has been the factors that leads to students' detachment with science as they proceed towards higher level. Secondary level of education is a prime level which decides students' future preference of stream at higher secondary and higher level. In Mizoram context the data of students' enrolment in science stream at higher education level indicate that student face a serious detachment from science owing to unfavourable classroom experiences at school, especially at secondary level. This calls for a serious need to look into the factors that might be the cause behind this disinterest. Contextualizing the background of Mizoram these finding are quite interesting as gender differences evident in educational output are very much confirming with the national scenario. However, as far as enrollment of girl child is concerned they are at par with their counter parts and also the sex ratio of the state is one of the healthiest in the country according to last census report (Census of India, 2011). Keeping these two backdrops in mind the researchers assumed that there would be no gender gap in the achievement levels of students in science, unlike the dominant national picture. But on the contrary both the variables of concern in the present study i.e. Emotional Stability and Achievement in Science seems to be favouring the male gender. This finding needs to be further investigated in relation to social contexts i.e. whether socio-cultural factors favour the male gender that subsequently acts an advantage for their better performances in sciences. Also, the emotional status of boys and girls differ that may also manifest as a factor to perform in science. The present finding is revealing a special insight into the Mizo adolescents' emotional profiles which also influence their relationship with the discipline of science. Science as a discipline need an emotional connect with the learner and more this connection is strengthen , it results in more desired outcome on part of learner whiling understanding, doing, philosophizing, and practicing science. Emotions are essential to be nurtured in science classroom in absence of which science is bound to be a dry, inert, boring which it is not. Science classroom experiences are actually very humorous, reactive and vibrant. One has to just change the perceptive. The new perspective states that emotions means a lot in manifestation of best within a human being and emotions govern learning and understanding of any kind. This truth holds true for teaching-learning contexts of science as well, in fact to a much larger extent than it was viewed in past through the contriving lens of cognition alone.

References

Abrahams, I. (2009). Does practical work really motivate? A study of the affective value of practical work in secondary school science. *International Journal of Science Education, 31*(17), 2335–2353.

Adi, Y., Killoran, A., Schrader McMillan, A., & Stewart-Brown, S. (2007).*Systematic review of interventions to promote mental wellbeing in primary schools.* Report 3.National Institute of Health and Clinical Excellence (NICE), London, UK.

Aleem, S. (2005). Emotional stability among college youth. *Journal of the Indian Academy of Applied Psychology*, *31*(1-2), 100-102.

Alsop, S. (2001). Seeking emotional involvement in science education: Food-chains and webs. *School Science Review*, *83*(302), 63–68.

Alsop, S., & Watts, M. (2003).Science education and affect. *International Journal of Science Education*, *25*(9), 1043-1047.

Barry, M. M., Clarke, A. M., Hussein, Y., Morreale, S., & Field, C. A. (2015). What works in enhancing social and emotional skills development during childhood and adolescence? A review of the evidence on the effectiveness of school-based and out- of-school programmes in the UK.

Berger, C., Alcalay, L., Torretti, A., &Milicic, N. (2011). Socio-emotional well-being and academic achievement: Evidence from a multilevel approach. *Psicologia: reflexao ecritica*, *24*(2), 344-351.

Brígido, M., Couso, D., Gutiérrez, C., &Mellado, V. (2013). The emotions about teaching and learning science: a study of prospective primary teachers in three spanish universities. *Journal of Baltic Science Education*, *12*(3).

Cattell, R. B., Eber, H. W., & Tatsuoka, M. M. (1970). *Handbook for the sixteen personality factor questionnaire (16 PF): In clinical, educational, industrial, and research psychology, for use with all forms of the test.* Institute for Personality and Ability Testing.

Census of India. (2011). Retrieved June 17,2019, from https://www.census2011.co.in/census/state/mizoram.html.

Chaturvedi, M. &Chander, R.(2010). The development of emotional stability scale, *Industrial Psychiatry Journal, 19*(1).

Eysenck, H. J. (1950). *Dimensions of personality* (Vol. 5).Transaction Publishers.

Goldberg, L. R. (1981). Language and individual differences: The search for universals in personality lexicons. *Review of personality and social psychology*, *2*(1), 141-165.

Guilford, J. P. (1979). *Cognitive psychology with a frame of reference*. Edits Pub. Hair, J.F., Hult, G.T.M., Ringle, C.M., Sarstedt, M. (2017). *A Primer on Partial Least Squares Structural Equation Modeling (PLS-SEM)* (2nd ed). Thousand Oaks, CA: Sage.

Hull, C. L. (1943). *Principles of behavior.* New York: Appleton-Century-Crofts.

Lal, K. (1968). *A comparative study of emotional stability of mentally superior and average adolescents*, Ph.D. Thesis (Edu.), Agra University.

McCrae, R. R., & John, O. P. (1992).An introduction to the fivefactor model and its applications. *Journal of personality*, *60*(2), 175-215.

Peck, D., & Whitlow, D. (1975). *Approaches to personality theory*. Methuen.

Pekrun, R., Goetz, T., &Titz, W. & Perry, R.P. (2002). Academic emotions in students' self regulated learning and achievement: A program of qualitative and quantitative research. *Educational Psychologist*, *37*, 91-106.

Reiss, M. J. (2005) Importance of affect in science education. In S. Alsop (Ed.) *Beyond Cartesian dualism: Encountering affect in the teaching and learning of science* (pp. 17–25). Dordrecht, The Netherlands: Springer.

Watts, M., & Alsop, S. (1997). A feeling for learning: modelling affective learning in school science. *The Curriculum Journal*, *8*(3), 351-365.

Chapter - VIII

The Role of Science Museums and Centres in Informal Science Education

— Lalrinkimi & Zairemtluangi

Introduction

Science museums, science centres and other institutions which are educational in nature, such as zoos, botanical gardens, aquariums, planetariums etc. have been widely reported to have a positive impact on education in the society. Many researchers (Anderson, 2000; Falk & Dierking, 2000; Renee & McClafferty, 1996) have concluded that these centres offer ambient learning atmospheres outside the confinement of a classroom. Interactive science centres are now regarded as educational and cultural resources which are focused on student learning and teacher professional development, and also promote an awareness of science amongst the general public (Morentin & Guisasola, 2014).They are fundamentally science communication centres wherein two approaches of communicating science are in operation – through exhibitions and activities. Various facets of contemporary science are displayed through exhibits, and activities are organized relevant to these themes. The social impact of science and technology are showcased using exhibits which are mostly interactive models, audio- visuals, computer-based models etc. According to MacDonald (1998), science centres are typically concerned with presenting universal abstract laws, principles, and phenomena. Phenomena are demonstrated, concepts are expounded and ideas are elicited using the displays. Exhibits are usually fabricated with the major intention of encouraging visitors to touch, think, feel and dream. The main objective of this paper is to highlight various infrastructural and instructional facilities existing at Mizoram Science Centre, Aizawl and the potential of these facilities in augmenting basic awareness of science to students in particular and also to the society as a whole.

Impact of Science Centres in Society

Science centres play a role in general improvement of public perception of science. A study by Falk and Needham (2010) reported that people who have visited their science centre believed that the science centre strongly influenced their science and technology understanding, attitudes and behaviours. This plays a role in increasing scientific temper among the people by helping to understand the basic laws of nature. There can be increased comprehension of scientific concepts linked to everyday lives and the immediate natural surroundings, thus helping to make changes in activities, habits and living standards towards achieving a healthy and sustainable future. All these are accomplished, apart from the general exhibitions, through various programs and sessions organized for targeted groups in the society, for example, students, teachers, the elderly, disabled persons, women community etc. Public engagement of various forms, will encourage people to think actively about science and understand its relevance to them in their daily lives, and will eventually inspire new champions for science research and encourage them to lobby for science (Pham, 2016). This concurs with other previous surveys which have reported increased knowledge and interest in conservation principles and general interest in science among science centre visitors and museum-goers (Adelman, Falk, & James, 2000; Garnett, 2001).In a study of attitudes toward animals conducted at the Birmingham Zoo, Bitgood (1992) reported that the less educated and less knowledgeable visitors appeared to benefit more from the visit in terms of positive attitude change since they increased their favourable ratings as a result of the visit, and also suggested that the zoo may have a favourable impact on the audience that needs the most persuasion (Bitgood, 1992, p. 10).

Science Centres Support and Complement Formal Science Education

Thornburgh (2017) stated that "since learning is both a product and a process that takes time and is different for everyone, informal science education could play a key role in advancing students' knowledge and attitudes towards science in formal education". Science centres often have a huge stream of school children visitors annually (Renee & McClafferty, 1996). Here, aspects of science are presented to the children unlike in nature, form or quality from those of formal educational institutions. For example, a spirit of biodiversity conservation and an anti-pollution mindset can be inculcated into young minds by using zoos, aquariums, botanical gardens etc. as environmental education tools. At the same time, specific topics in school curriculum can be dealt with using other activities such as science workshops, science demonstration lectures, seminars etc. A study by Sasson (2014) concluded that the academic science center activities positively affect scientific thinking skills of students with a significant improvement in the students' inquiry and graphing skills. In the study, students were reported to have significantly improved in their ability to ask research questions based on reading scientific texts, and to describe and analyze research results that were presented graphically.

Mizoram Science Centre

The science policies of Govt. of India have shown emphasis on nurturing a science and technology literate society as shown by Science, Technology & Innovation (STI) Policy, 2013. Ministry of Culture, Govt. of India is setting up Science Cities, Science Centres and Innovation Hubs across India using National Council of Science Museums (NCSM) as the implementing agency. The various science centres in north-eastern region of India were also initiated during the 1990's. Currently, there are 47 science museums/centres spread across the country and others like Mobile Science Exhibition (MSE) units for rural areas etc. (ncsm.gov.in). Science Centres under NCSM encompass several objectives including creating awareness and enhancing public understanding in the process of science and technology, to supplement science education given in schools and colleges and to promote out-of school educational activities to enhance scientific enquiry and creativity among the students.

Mizoram Science Centre (MSC) is located at Berawtlang, Zemabawk, Aizawl. It covers an area of 23.057 sq km, and is situated between 92°45' 52.45 E longitudes and 23°43' 54.84 N latitudes. The Centre was set up by NCSM and Government of Mizoram and was opened on 26th July, 2003. It is the only institution of its kind for the state of Mizoram. The Centre has been visited by a number of students, teachers and general visitors. The exhibit items are placed indoors and outdoors depending on the nature of exhibits. Majority of the exhibits have been designed and fabricated by NCSM to fulfil the various objectives formulated for science centres under NCSM.

Outdoor Science Park at MSC

The outdoor science park has a general theme of 'science brought outside the boundary of four walls'. A number of exhibits which are recreational in nature such as swings, see-saw, echo-tube, tug of war, lift yourself, musical tubes, elliptical speaking tube, etc., are attractively presented, each of which have their own scientific concepts and learning objectives. The exhibits portray diverse principles and concepts of science including sound (sound waves, reflection of sound, speed of sound), force (pulley system, lever), pendulum (oscillations, potential and kinetic energy), speed (velocity and acceleration), Newton's third law of motion, reflective property of an ellipse, etc.,

Table 8.1: Some Exhibits Present in Outdoor Science Park of MSC

Exhibit	*Scientific Concept / Learning Objective*
Swing & Sympathetic Swing	Pendulum Concept; Oscillations
Action and Reaction	Newton's Third Law of Motion
See-Saw	Lever; Fulcrum (Centred and Off-Centred)
Echo Tube	Sound Waves; Reflected sound
Elliptical Speaking Tube	Reflective Property of an Ellipse
Lift Yourself	Force; Pulley Systems
Lever Reduces Effort	Levers Help in Reducing Effort to Do Any Work
Tug of War	Pulley Block Gives a Mechanical Advantage
Velocity and Acceleration	Acceleration of Bodies; Gravitational Force
Musical Tubes	Pitch of Sound Varies with Length in Freely Hung Tubes
Win the Race	Speeds of Wheels; Mass Distribution

Exhibit Galleries at MSC

The indoor exhibit areas are organized into Forest Gallery and Fun Science Galleries. The Forest Gallery has an assortment of visual and graphical interpretations of aspects related to forests, ranging from the structure of forest ecosystems, functions of forests, forest products etc. Special emphasis has been given on selected snakes and fish species of Mizoram, specifically highlighting several fish species described from Mizoram. They serve a dual purpose of knowledge enrichment as well as a motivational role for students.

Table 8.2: Some Exhibits Present in Forest Gallery of MSC

Exhibit Item	*Scientific Concept / Learning Objective*
World Forest Cover	Global Forest Distribution
Forest For Life	Food Chain and Trophic Levels
Plant Evolution	Life Cycles Angiosperms of Mosses, Ferns, Gymnosperms,
Age of a Tree, Value of a Tree	Summer Wood, Spring Wood
Photosynthesis	Process, Raw-Materials and Products of Photosynthesis
Forest Ecosystem	Grazing Food Web; Detritus Food Web
Coal Formation	Coal Formation; Fossils
Some Snakes and Fish Species of Mizoram	Local Names and Scientific Names of Species; Toxicity Levels of Snake Venoms; Species Described from Mizoram

The Fun Science Galleries are equipped with interactive displays and hands-on experimental activities that cover several aspects of science. The exhibits like 'Is light visible? Changing colours, colour pyramid, leave your shadows behind etc. are based on concepts of light. Exhibits based on concepts of sound include visualizing sound, organ pipes, electronic organ, Seebeck's siren, coded music, etc. Principles of electricity and magnetism are also shown in fun ways using exhibits like lazy channel, hand battery and Curie point. In addition to these, a diverse range of scientific theories on optical illusion, vacuum, mirrors, planetary motion, etc. are presented in attractive ways to enable students to learn science through fun and enjoyment.

Table 8.3: Some Exhibits Present in Fun Science Galleries of MSC

Exhibit Item	*Scientific Concept / Learning Objective*
Is Light Visible?	Nature of Light
Changing Colours	Polarized Light
Organ Pipes	Vibration of Air; Pitch of Sound
Cone Runs Uphill	Centre of Gravity of a Cone
Illusion with a Ring	Optical Illusion
2D to 3D	2D and 3D Objects
Vortex	Fluid Velocity; Conservation of Angular Momentum
Planetary Motion	Elliptical Paths of Planets; Gravitational Field of Sun
Electronic Organ	Activation of a Series of Electronic Oscillator Circuits when Reeds are Touched by Hand to Produce Music
Seebeck's Siren	Movement of Air through Holes to Produce Sound
The Acrobatic Stick	Hyperbola
The Impossible Mixture	Immiscible Liquids; Density
Curie Point	Magnetism
Hand Battery	Electricity
Lazy Channel	Electricity; Magnetism

(*Contd...*)

Spinning Eraser	Induced Blindness
Coded Music	Binary Codes; Optical Sensor
Visualizing Sound	Vibration; Sound Waves; Frequency
Colour Pyramid	Primary and Secondary Colours
Leave your Shadow Behind	Phosphorescence

Space Education Centre at MSC

A comprehensive study done by Thornburgh (2017) concluded that the immersive environment and unique capabilities of a digital planetarium positively influenced students' attitudes, learning, retention and thinking. The Space Education Centre at MSC has a digital planetarium which is an influential tool for propagating astronomical knowledge. The dynamic sky and the outer space environment are simulated in the theatre for astronomy popularization, simultaneously making scientific knowledge accessible and enjoyable. Audio-visual planetarium programs portraying various aspects of the solar system and the surrounding space in the universe are being screened for public viewing at Space Education Centre. The planetarium is an exceptional instrument for teaching concepts related to astronomy and geography and people of all ages are made to be aware of the marvelous spectacle of the night sky. Additionally, the multimedia kiosks and poster displays also serve as educational tools for all visitors.

Innovation Hub

The Innovation Hub has been set up by NCSM under the Scheme for Promoting Innovation, Creativity and Engagement in Science (SPICES) approved by Planning Commission and Ministry of Culture, Govt. of India. The main objectives of the Innovation Hub are to equip and strengthen activities of the Science Centre, to inspire innovations by young children, to catalyze creation of more innovation hubs in different parts of the country especially in rural areas and to provide appropriate environment to nurture creative and innovating ideas of young children. The Innovation Hub of MSC has innovative laboratories including physics, chemistry, biology, mechanical, electrical and electronics laboratories. Other sections like educational robotics section, 3d-printer section and the thod-phod-jod (break apart and build) section are intended for shaping and nurturing young minds for development in technical innovation. A study by Ospennikova, Ershov, & Iljin (2015) has also particularly emphasized the implementation of educational robotics as an efficient tool to inspire technical creativity for fostering the future generation of engineers and inventors. According to them, graduates of modern school have to be prepared to life activity and in connection to this, new and quite complex educational objectives must be set to secondary school: (1) updating the content of polytechnic education of students, taking into account such areas as robotics technology innovation; (2) targeted training of future consumers of robotic environment services; (3) introduction to preparation of future robotic systems manufacturers- research engineers, design engineers, planning engineers (Ospennikova et al, 2015, p. 19).

Science Popularization Prospects of Science Centres

Besides the various existing infrastructural facilities which provide hands-on opportunity of 'doing science', a science centre has the potential for hosting scientific awareness programs like organizing conferences, seminars, public debates etc. on current scientific events (such as prevailing contagious diseases, astronomical events like solar and lunar eclipses etc.). Observation of important days of scientific relevance e.g., National Science Day, World Environment Day, National Nutrition Week, etc. with selected communities of the society is also a major feature of science centres. Organizing Science fairs and Science exhibitions designed exclusively for students of different age levels have played a momentous role in shaping young minds for science-related endeavours in the later stages of life. Many great innovative ideas have been reported to have stemmed from students' participations in such events, and also from the activities in the Innovation Hubs of the science centres in India.

Challenges for Mizoram Science Centre

A considerable number of reports have demonstrated the positive role of science centres and museums in complementing formal science education. However, there is a complete lack of a systematic study regarding the actual effects of Mizoram Science Centre on the student science learning scenario in Mizoram. Only a nonfigurative and abstract impact can be drawn at this time. A variety of research projects by science education researchers need to be undertaken keeping in view both the educational and societal impact of the centre to the surrounding community. Moreover, proposals and suggestions also need to be worked out to enhance the efficacy of the centre in relation to its fundamental objectives.

Apart from these, financial constraints need to be addressed in order to augment the infrastructures and accessible amenities of the centre to cater to the growing needs of the student communities. The centre also needs to take concrete steps, in addition to the current activities, to enhance the effectiveness of student visits to the galleries, innovation hub and digital planetarium to fully utilize their potential in complementing science education.

Conclusion and Recommendations for Enhancing the Effectiveness of School Visits to Science Centres

Even though school visits and field trips to museums and science centres constitute a powerful learning resource, visits need to be integrated into classroom programming to optimize learning (Morentin & Guisasola, 2014). Field trips can enhance learning, promote student interest and complement school-based instruction, but the teacher's pedagogical practices and the learning agendas set up for their students are essential to achieve the intended learning objectives (Davidson, Passmore, & Anderson, 2010). Interestingly, school visits to such centres can be completely off-track and unproductive in the absence of proper planning and supervision from the teachers, and at times can solely become a fun activity rather than an educational experience. Suitable methodologies encompassing the below- mentioned proposals could be adopted prior to school visits to science centres and museums:

1. Meticulous planning by teachers to pursue out-of school learning objectives ideally corresponding to syllabi and curriculums. Teachers may take the effort to familiarize themselves with the exhibits and the general atmosphere of the museum or centre with the intention of imparting structured guidance to the students.
2. Discussion between teachers and personnel of a particular centre/ museum/zoo/ aquarium/planetarium etc. prior to a visit to produce specific learning outcomes.
3. Groupings among students for assessment purposes. Pre-visit and Post-visit assessments may prove valuable but the nature of assessment may be made variable to suit the age groups of the students. Post-visit competitions among the student groups in the form of scientific poster writings, write-ups, quizzes, photography and sketching competitions etc. relevant to the encountered exhibits may generate interest and motivation among the pupils.
4. Organizing teachers' scientific training by the centres. Providing training to groups of teachers whose institutions would be utilizing the resources of a particular centre may prove beneficial.
5. To employ "visitor empowering tools and strategies such as – information for planning a visit on the web site, handouts/guides

in the lobby or exhibit halls, video demonstrations, tour guide instructing visitors how to view exhibits and providing strategies, e.g., games, questions to formulate" (Bitgood, 2015, p.41).

References

Adelman, L., Falk, J., & James, S. (2000). Impact of National Aquarium in Baltimore on visitor's conservation attitudes, behavior, and knowledge. *Curator*, *43*, 33-61. https://doi.org/10.1111/j.2151-6952.2000.tb01158.x

Anderson, D., Lucas, K.B., Ginns, I.S., & Dierkng, L.D. (2000). Development of knowledge about electricity and magnetism during a visit to a science museum and related post- visit activites. *Science Education*, *84*(5), 658–679. https://doi.org/10.1002/1098-237X(200009)84:5<658::AID-SCE6>3.0.CO;2-A

Bitgood, S. (1992). The impact of a zoo visit on attitudes: A preliminary report on interaction effects. *Visitor Behavior*, *7*(3), 7.

Bitgood, S. (2015). Empower visitors to maximize the value of their visit. *JVA Interp News,* pp. 38-41.

Davidson, S. K., Passmore, C., & Anderson, D. (2010). Learning on zoo field trips: The interaction of the agendas and practices of students, teachers and zoo educators. *Science Education*, *94* (1), 122–141.

Falk, J. H., & Dierking, L. D. (2000). *Learning from museums: Visitor experiences and the making of meaning.* Walnut Creek, CA: Altamira Press.

Falk, J.H., & Needham, M.D. (2010). Measuring the Impact of a Science Center on its Community. *Journal of Research in Science Teaching, 48*(1), 1-12. https://doi.org/10.1002/tea.20394

Garnett, R. (2002). *The Impact of Science Centers/Museums on their Surrounding Communities*: Summary Report. Canberra, Australia: Questacon. www.astc.org/resource/case/Impact-study02.pdf

Macdonald, S. (1998). *The politics of display: Museums, science, culture.* New York, NY: Routledge.

Morentin, N., & Guisasola, J. (2015).The role of science museum field trips in the primary teacher preparation. *International Journal of Science and Mathematics Education, 13*(5), 965-990. https://doi.org/10.1007/s10763-014-9522-4

Ospennikova, E., Ershov, M., & Iljin, I. (2015). Educational robotics as an innovative educational technology. *Social and Behavioral Sciences, 214*, 18-26. doi:10.1016/j.sbspro.2015.11.588

Pham, D. (2016). Public engagement is key for the future of science research. *Npj Science of Learning*, *1*, 16010; doi:10.1038/npjscilearn.2016.10

Rennie, L., & McClafferty, T. (1995). Using visits to interactive science and technology centers, museums, aquaria, and zoos to promote learning in science. *Journal of Science Teacher Education*, *6*(4), 175-185. https://doi.org/10.1007/BF02614639

Sasson, I. (2014). The role of informal science centres in science education: attitudes, skills, and self-efficacy. *Journal of Technology and Science Education*, *4*(3), 167-189. http://dx.doi.org/10.3926/jotse.123

Thornburgh, W.R. (2017).The role of the planetarium in students' attitudes, learning, and thinking about astronomical concepts. *Electronic Theses and Dissertations*. Paper 2684. https://doi.org/10.18297/etd/2684

Chapter - IX

A Study on the Science Promotion Wing of the State Council of Educational Research and Training of Mizoram

— *Lynda Zohmingliani*

Introduction

The Science Promotion Wing was set up as a separate department under the Directorate of School Education as per the dictates of the Government of India and was initially headed by a Science Promotion Officer, later on designated as Deputy Director in the year 1988. It was an exercise to implement a UNICEF project. Initially, the Wing operated almost entirely with the help of funds received from the UNICEF. The Project, intended to strengthen science education at the elementary stage was immediately carried out in 50 primary as well as 30 middle schools. At present the Science Promotion Wing is attached to SCERT as the Department of Science and Mathematics. It proudly continues to be the main promoter of science and mathematics throughout the state of Mizoram. It works on the lines of the following objectives:

1. To review the existing curriculum in science and mathematics in order to generate a taste for learning.
2. To enhance teachers' professional competence by arranging suitable training programmes for teachers in science and mathematics from primary to higher secondary level.

3. To provide necessary equipment in science and mathematics laboratories for practical as well as demonstration purposes.
4. To train and encourage teachers to conduct demonstration of scientific experiments and mathematical concepts using inexpensive and indigenous equipment and materials besides laboratory work.
5. Provision for co-curricular activities such as organization of Science Exhibitions, Seminars, Eastern India Science Fair etc. for promoting students interest as well as academic achievement in these subjects.
6. To provide incentive to meritorious students in the form of cash awards for proficiency in science and mathematics on the basis of public and promotion examinations.

1. Allocation of Funds to Science Promotion Wing

After the UNICEF project was terminated, the state government took the mantle of giving financial support to the Science Promotion Wing on a yearly basis. This has enabled the wing to carry on its work to promote science education at the school level throughout the state.

Table-9.1 shows that the state government had been steadily increasing its financial support to the Science Promotion Wing so as to enable this wing to continue its various activities to generate and maintain interest in science education among students at the secondary level. However, the amount sanctioned includes staff salary as well. Therefore, in consideration if the importance of science education, it is not a huge sum of money by any standards. Moreover, a large percentage is from the planned budget. All these show that this department could do with a boost in budget if the state is to show marked development in science education.

Table 9.1: State Allocation for Science Promotion Wing (1987-2008)

Year	*Budget (in lakhs)*		*Actual Expenditure (in lakhs)*	
	Plan	*Non-Plan*	*Plan*	*Non-Plan*
2012 - 2013	64.34	82.24	64.34	82.24
2013 - 2014	96.20	68.70	68.73	97.19
2014 - 2015	117.45	30.40	30.40	117.45
2015 - 2016	117.30	18.00	34.00	115.41
2016 -2017	129.45	36.50	No data	No data

Source: Demands for Grant, Govt. of Mizoram.

2. Staffing

The Wing is at present, taken care of by a total of 11 staff. The placement of staff during the time this investigation was made is reflected in table-9.2. As can be seen from the table, a number of positions are still vacant.

A close study of Table-9.2 reveals that there are some posts that are still left vacant. The most obvious weakness in the wing is that the top post is not vacant but is taken up as an additional charge. Besides this, in view of the fact that only 3 posts were filled up for 4 posts for science consultants, 1 in place of 2 posts for computer operator and other posts that are not filled by permanent staff, it was clear that this wing had not been fully attended to as it deserved to be. There are vacancies which have existed ten years before which still exist today. All these show that this department has been quite neglected in spite of the importance of its position.

Table 9.2: Staffing Position in Science Promotion Wing

Designation	*Post(s) Sanctioned*	*Post(s) Filled*	*Vacancies*
Deputy Director	1	1	-
Science Consultant	4	3	1
Programmer	1	1	-
Assistant Programmer	1	1	-
Computer Operator	2	1	1
Laboratory Assistant	1	1	-
Laboratory Attendant	1	1	-
Laboratory Bearer	1	-	1
Science Supervisor	2	1	-
Projectionist	1	1	-
Peon	2	-	2
Driver	2	2	-
Total	**20**	**11**	**5**

Source: Field Visit.

3. Programmes and Activities for Science Promotion Wing

Although the UNICEF project is no more, the Science Promotion Wing continues to make the scientific dreams of youngsters in Mizoram a reality. Some of the major activities carried out in order to implement the objectives of the Science Promotion Wing have been listed under the following heads:

(i) Training of Science and Mathematics Teachers

Trainings were considered even more vital for teacher development since the adoption of CBSE syllabus from session 2001. As shown by office records, Science Promotion Wing had been diligently organizing training programs for science and mathematics teachers. But may be due to lack of funds, the training programmes had not been organized every year. Besides this, the number of science teachers and mathematics teachers was not specified. So the investigator could not be sure whether the same number of science and mathematics teachers received annual training or not.

(ii) Supply of Science Kits and Science Equipments

As shown by Table-9.3, which shows the number of schools that were covered within a period of ten years (2013-2017), the Science Promotion Wing has been steadily supplying science kits to secondary and higher secondary schools on a yearly basis. However, the number of schools covered is much less than the actual number of schools in the state. Since most of the scientific equipment is perishable items, a yearly supply of equipment for science laboratory is a necessity and not a luxury. Moreover, schools do not receive regular supplies. This is a sad picture considering the importance of scientific equipment for the development of science laboratories. In this regard, it is important for the schools and the Science Promotion Wing to have a proper dialogue so that there is a proper understanding between them.

Table 9.3: Supply of Science Kits and Science Equipments by the Science Promotion Wing

Year	*Secondary Schools Supplied*	*Higher Secondary Schools supplied*
2012-2013	100	15
2013-2014	100	15
2014-2015	100	15
2015-2016	100	15
2016-2017	-	-

Source: SCERT Annual Reports.

(iii) Organisation of Science Exhibitions

With the noble intention to develop scientific temper in students the wing has been organizing a state level science exhibition, sponsored by NCERT, New Delhi and Science Technology and Environmental Council, Mizoram, since the last 30 years. The winner of this exhibition is sent to represent the state at the national level science exhibition.

(iv) Eastern India Science Fair

The Wing has been successfully organizing Eastern India Science Fair Seminar every year in collaboration with Birla Industrial and Technological

Museum. Although it has not been possible for all students to participate, the number of students who do participate come back with positive feedbacks regarding the fair. It would be ideal to cover a larger group of students each year so as to expose them to scientific technology.

(v) Holding of Science Seminar

The Science Promotion Wing in collaboration with Birla Industrial and Technological Museum, Kolkata, has been organizing a district and state level science seminar every year. The best performer in the seminar is recommended for participation in the National Level Science Seminar, New Delhi. Students are encouraged to express their views on subjects of topical and academic interests.

(vi) Cash Awards

The School Education Department has a provision of cash award as incentive to meritorious students of primary, middle and high school students for their proficiency in science and mathematics. The award is based on their performance in board examination at PSE, MSLC, and HSLC and promotion examination of class VIII and IX. Table-9.4 gives a detail of the number of students who have received cash awards during the years 2012 to 2017.

Table 9.4: Numbers of Students Given the Cash Awards by the Science Promotion Wing (2012-2017)

Year	*Numbers of Students Given Cash Awards*
2012-2013	94
2013-2014	87
2014-2015	1110
2015-2016	142
2016-2017	120
Total	**1553**

Source: SCERT Annual Reports.

A look at Table-9.4 reveals that The Science Promotion Wing had been organizing cash awards for its meritorious students almost on a yearly basis. However, it does not clearly specify the number of middle school, high school and higher secondary school students who had received the award. But even without this knowledge, a total of 1553 is a small number if it is for a span of 5 years and covering three levels of education.

(vii) Improvement and Establishment of Science Laboratories

The Wing, depending on the availability of funds, provides fund to schools to build their science laboratories and furniture. However, there have been years when no school was assisted as no separate fund was allocated by the state government, to the wing for this purpose. But no clear data is available on this.

(viii) Centrally Sponsored Schemes for Improvement of Science Education in Schools

This Centrally Sponsored Scheme for Improvement of Science Education in Schools, introduced in Mizoram since 1987-88 had the following components:

(a) **Provision of Science Kits, Equipments and Library Books to Schools**: The Science Promotion Wing reserves certain funds under the Centrally Sponsored Scheme to provide better scientific equipments to schools. Besides this, library books are also supplied with a view to broaden the students' outlook.

(b) **Organisation of Training Programme for Science and Mathematics Teachers of Various Categories of Schools in Mizoram under the Scheme**: The Centrally sponsored scheme also covered the training of teacher but a detailed account was not made available through the annual report of achievements.

(c) **State Level Drama Competition**: This is also held every year and students and teachers from the state secondary and higher secondary schools enthusiastically participate. Each year, different themes are selected for which awards are given to best performers.

(ix) INSPIRE (Innovation in Science Pursuit for Inspired Research)

This is a flagship programme of the Ministry of Science and Technology, Government of India. It has five components covering te entire range of education. A one-time award of Rs. 5000/- is given to students out of which they would spend 50% in the building of a suitable model for exhibition and the rest 50% for transportation. The scheme had a budget of Rs. 79,45,000/- which is to be spent on 1589 students during the 11th five year plan. The scheme was revamped as INSPIRE MANAK in the year 2017. In the said year, a sum Rs. 10000/- each, was distributed to 21 students in preparation for their exhibition.

Conclusion

Besides the activities that have been discussed, the Science Promotion Wing is also actively involved in the revision of textbooks as well as running a competent computer cell. It can be concluded that as far as conduction of yearly readymade activities is concerned, the Science Promotion Wing has done its best to promote Science education among students of Mizoram. However, it is also glaringly obvious that only a small percentage of the schools and students are covered each year. On the other hand, the funds allotted to the wing is sparing at best. Especially in consideration of the fact the funds include staff salary is small by any standard for a state of the size of Mizoram. Considering its important role in the overall development of the state, it would be worthwhile for the state government to give more opportunities and incentives for this Wing to fill up vacant posts, perform better in its activities and generally strive to make science education at the school level as progressive as possible.

References

Zohmingliani, L. (2016). Status of Science Education in the north east: A study of Mizoram. Mittal Publications, New Delhi.

Demands for Grants (2012-2013). Government of Mizoram. Demands for Grants (2013-2014), Government of Mizoram. Demands for Grants (2014-2015), Government of Mizoram.

Demands for Grants (2015-2016). Government of Mizoram. Demands for Grants (2016-2017), Government of Mizoram.

Annual Report (2012-2013). State Council of Educational Research and Training, Government of Mizoram Annual Report (2012-2013), State Council of Educational Research and Training, Government of Mizoram.

Annual Report (2012-2013). State Council of Educational Research and Training, Government of Mizoram.

Annual Report (2013-2014). State Council of Educational Research and Training, Government of Mizoram.

Annual Report (2014-2015). State Council of Educational Research and Training, Government of Mizoram.

Annual Report (2015-2016). State Council of Educational Research and Training, Government of Mizoram.

Annual Report (2016-2017). State Council of Educational Research and Training, Government of Mizoram.

About the Editor and Contributors

The Editor

Nithiya Amirtham S is an assistant professor at Department of Education, Mizoram University (Central University), Aizawl, Mizoram, India. Her research interest includes STEM education, gender and education, higher education and teacher education. Currently she has been supervising two doctoral research scholars working in the area of higher education and STEM education.

The Contributors

Poonam Agrawal is distinguished professor and former head of Gender Studies at National Council of Educational Research and Training (NCERT), New Delhi. She holds a post- doctorate degree in Bio-Chemistry and has more than 30 years experience on various responsible positions in Universities (in India and abroad), ministry, research institutes in India & abroad and NCERT involving research, teaching, administration, planning and coordination, development, training, extension, guidance and monitoring. In NCERT she has worked as Professor and Head, since 1995 of four Departments/Divisions, namely, Division for vocations in Home Science, Department of Women's Studies, International Relations Division, Department of Educational Research and Policy Perspectives and also worked as Joint Director of PSS Central Institute of Vocational Education.

Amardeep Kumar is a doctoral candidate at National Institute of Educational Planning and Administration (NIEPA), New Delhi. His areas of interests are Higher Education, Policy of Positive Discrimination, Equity and Social Justice, Education of Disadvantaged and Aspirations. Besides he has interest in labour and development, migration and diaspora. He is a founder member of Global Research Forum on Diaspora and

Transnationalism (GRFDT). He is also a lifetime member of Comparative Education Society of India (CESI), affiliated with the World Council of Comparative Education Societies (WCCES).

Lalduhsanga Pachuau is currently serving as assistant professor at the Department of Pharmaceutical Sciences, Assam University. He is an alumnus of Dibrugarh University, Assam and former Assistant Professor at Regional Institute of Paramedical and Nursing Sciences, Aizawl. He has been teaching Pharmacy course over the last 10 years and his area of research is in the development of novel drug delivery systems, natural products and biomaterials. He has published more than 20 research and review papers in reputed international journals, wrote 10 book chapters and presented his research at various international and national conferences. He is a life member of Indian Science Congress Association, Asian Polymer Association and Society of Pharmaceutical Education and Research, and a recipient of several recognitions and fellowships at national and international levels.

Mrinmoy Acharjee a graduate from Department of Pharmaceutical Sciences, Assam University in 2018 and studied the history of pharmacy education in North-East India.

Tapojyoti Das a pharmacy graduate from Department of Pharmaceutical Sciences, Assam University in 2018 worked in the area of history of pharmacy education in North-East India.

Ferrando Lyngdoh Nonglait is a senior research fellow in the Department of Education, North Eastern Hill University (NEHU), Shillong. His area of interest is Education of Rural Students. He is the Recipient of S. C. Dutta Memorial Award for academic excellence from Shillong College in 2014 and is also the recipient of U Kiang Nongbah Memorial Award for excellence in academics and for rendering service to people from North- Eastern Hill University in 2016.

Euodia B. Myrthong is presently an assistant professor at Department of Education, North Eastern Hill University (NEHU), Shillong. Her specializations are Research Methodology, Mental Health Education, Educational Psychology and Guidance and Counselling. She had presented many papers and had also written papers related to these subjects and have conducted workshops on Innovative teaching practices. She had also provided lectures in UGC-HRDC NEHU, Shillong as well as in various schools and colleges concerning the Innovative teaching practices as well as in Research Methodology.

Lalmuanzuali is currently working as assistant professor at Department of Education, Mizoram University, Aizawl and has 13 years of teaching experience at post-graduate level. Her doctoral research is on science education which was a comparative study between Mizoram and Meghalaya states of India. She is also interested in educational & vocational guidance and special education fields.

H. Malsawmi is professor and head of Department of Education, Mizoram University, Aizawl. She has 36 years of teaching and 14 years of research experience in higher education. Her area of specialization includes educational psychology, special education and educational measurement & evaluation.

Nitu Kaur has been serving as an assistant professor in the Department of Education, Mizoram University, Aizawl, Mizoram since 2015. She has the experience of teaching both at undergraduate and post graduate levels. Her research work is based on the impact of some affective variables on students' achievement in science. The role of affective domain in science has been a neglected arena of research until very lately when the connections between them have been stressed out. Her research work tries to explain a similar connection in context of Mizoram. Her areas of interest in research are that of science education, research methodology and curriculum development.

R. P. Vadhera is distinguished professor and former head of the Department of Education, Mizoram University and presently serving as the pro-vice chancellor of Mizoram University. He completed his higher education from Kurukshetra University, Haryana. He is a veteran educationist with teaching experience of more than thirty years in North-Eastern Hill and Mizoram University. He has an expertise in field of research methodology, advance educational statistics, educational planning & management, curriculum development and economics of education. He is specialist in north-eastern perspectives in education due to his long association with this region of the country. He has been nominated as Mizoram state nodal officer for monitoring national programs of SSA. He has the credit of guiding several research thesis and dissertations. He is the author of several works in the field of education and associated with many educational institutions and research organization. He has conducted many research programmes, refresher courses in the field of research methods and teacher education.

Lalrinkimi is currently working as education assistant at Mizoram Science Centre, Berawtlang, Aizawl, Mizoram and completed her doctoral studies from the Department of Botany, Mizoram University, Aizawl. Her research focus was on algae biology. She had attended and presented papers in national and international conferences. She has several years of experience in teaching science subject at various levels, and is keenly interested in imparting informal science education to students and general public through various activities of the science centre.

Zairemtluangi is an associate professor at the Department of Education, Government. J. Thankima College, Aizawl, Mizoram. She has several years of teaching experience as a senior faculty in the department. She had attended and presented papers in national and international conferences and is currently conducting research on emotional maturity and parental encouragement among college students in Aizawl District, Mizoram.

Lynda Zohmingliani has been a faculty of Department of education, Mizoram University, for the last 15 years. She served as a Secondary science teacher under the government of Mizoram for 9 years before she entered the university as a faculty. She has done her research on science education and also published a book on the same topic. She is also interested in environmental studies as well as higher education in India.

Index